WEALTH KUNG FU

VOL 2
UNFUCK YOUR MIND

T E N   R E P S

Notice of Rights

Disclaimer

This book is intended for informational and educational purposes only. The information presented in this book is not a substitute for professional financial or legal advice. The author and publisher make no representations or warranties of any kind, express or implied, about the completeness, accuracy, reliability, suitability or availability with respect to the book or the information, products, services or related graphics contained in the book for any purpose. Any reliance you place on such information is therefore strictly at your own risk.

The author may include affiliate links in this book. If you purchase a product or service through one of these links, the author may receive a commission. The presence of affiliate links does not affect the content or recommendations made in this book. The author only includes affiliate links for products or services that they believe will add value to the reader.

Please consult with a professional financial advisor or attorney before making any financial decisions. The

ABOUT
THE AUTHOR

TEN REPS is a writer, creative director, film director, brand strategist and managing partner of an advertising agency. He has 23 years of experience under his belt as a private investor in real estate, equities, precious metals, bitcoin, crypto, and alternative assets. He has taken his share of proverbial punches, bruises and KOs as well as victories, all suffered or celebrated in private. **Wealth Kung Fu** draws from his own unique experience.

He is fully cognisant of the reality that all the wealth and investment books he has ever read in his lifetime were, while informative and helpful, dead serious and some were even boring as fuck. He hopes his literary contribution as author will add a bit of spark in the category through his casual, conversational style of writing. He aspires to turn the attention of his readers to emerging disruptions from new technologies that are redefining the assets landscape. He imagines we are in unchartered territory and for the investor, unprecedented opportunities are presenting themselves like never before.

FOREWORD

Given a wish between being poor or rich, no one in their right mind would choose to be poor. Being poor can lead people to do desperate and downright insidious things.

Being poor sucks. I know. I was there.

I grew up in a lower middle class family with very little at our disposal. Family harmony and happiness were constantly decimated by money problems, exacerbated by a non-ceasing compulsive gambling problem, constant borrowing, and zero money management skill. It's a childhood I never want to return to.

Observing the poor whom I personally know, my thoughts often drift to the one colossal attribute they have: the absence of financial literacy.

I draw solely from my own experience, perceptions, and knowledge to write this series of books.
My main goal is to help those without financial education to learn. And in doing that, I try to make the writing entertaining, in the belief that it's easier to educate after we have first entertained.

Clearly, my writing style is intended for those with a sense of self-deprecating humour. For the easily offended, please have the balls to go through it, if you must, with the knowledge that I am not a slave to political correctness, which is the same thing as censorship. Fuck that shit.

Happy reading.

Wealth Kung Fu Vol 2: Unfuck Your Mind

Table of Content

Chapter 14: Modern Investment Assets

Chapter 15: Investing

Chapter 16: The Myths of Investing

Chapter 17: $10,000 to $10,000,000!

Chapter 18: Daily Habits of the Unfucked Mind

Chapter 19: The Winners Portfolio

Chapter 20: Staying Wealthy and Unfucked from hereon

Introduction:

Unleashing the Power of Wealth Kung Fu

Welcome, wealth-seeking warrior, to the temple of knowledge – **Wealth Kung Fu**. Get ready to learn, unlearn and relearn in an age where not being able to do so would render one illiterate in this rapidly-changing digital epoch. But try to do so with a mirthful spirit of positivity, grounded in the sobriety of knowledge.

We continue our journey from where we left off in **Wealth Kung Fu Vol 1 – Zero To 1 Million** Chapters 1 – 10. This book starts from Chapter 11. We hope you leaf through the pages while snacking on your dumplings as we prepare you for the journey ahead.

Here at **Wealth Kung Fu**, we're all about being composed during the yin-yang bifurcations of the markets, but also ready to act and strike with courage during dips and crashes, just like a clever Kung Fu master knows when to roundhouse kick a baddie to oblivion.

We shall attempt to break down complex financial mumbo-jumbo into simple everyday syntax and try to keep things grounded for ease of comprehension. Sniff the aroma of freshly brewed currencies and sip from a cup that's runneth over.

So, fasten your Kung Fu belt and prepare to get into the martial arts of wealth-building. Try to be patient like a Zen monk, meditating in Zen-like calmness through market ups and downs. Your Kung Fu grade discipline can defeat the madness of market upheavals as you ride your pet dragon in your quest for life-changing wealth.

Investing can be a wild ride, and it can sometimes seem like the investor has to take action like a bull in a China shop (but with more grace, of course). But without **Wealth Kung Fu**, you will never roundhouse kick those money worries away and hear the "Ka-Ching!" new all-time highs bring.

Step into the temple of **Wealth Kung Fu**, where warriors kick and punch their way to good monetary health. Let's flip dollars like Jackie Chan flips bad guys and turn those soggy, soft fiat currencies into hard money and sound assets. Brace yourself for an epic adventure in the world of wealth-building and learn how wealth can soar like a majestic dragon in the sky.

KNOWLEDGE
BUYS YOU INCOME.

INCOME
BUYS YOU ASSETS.

ASSETS
BUY YOU FREEDOM.

Chapter 11:

That Loser Mindset

Being poor or rich starts with a state of mind. The poor and middle class have mindsets that are very different from the rich. It is best you learn both sets in order to know which to avoid and which to adopt. Once you do so, you will undoubtedly realize that you have indeed been programmed to think like a poor or middle-class person. The Matrix wants you to do its biddings. This kind of poor and middle-class programme is actually a mindfuck. Realizing you have been mindfucked all along can only be good for you. Once you know what you don't know, it is time to unfuck your own mind.

POOR
MINDSET

Success Unimportant

Blames Others

Spends Money

Refuses to Study

Attention on the Past

Thinks Small

Fears Change

Victim Mindset

Criticizes

Wastes Time

Causes Problems

Single Flow of Income

Work-Driven

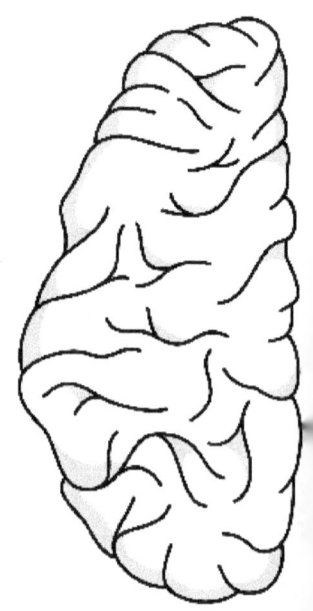

RICH
MINDSET

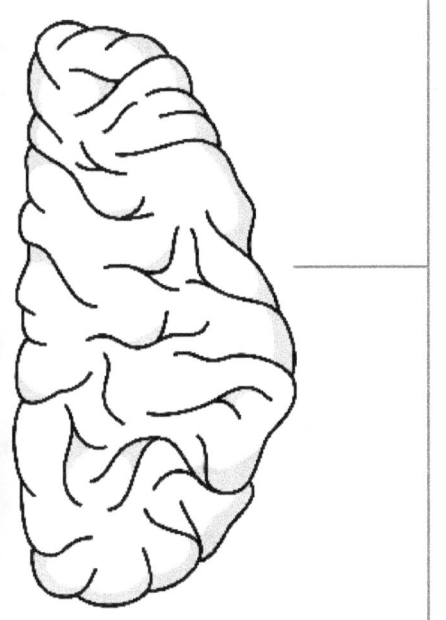

Success is Obligation

Responsible

Invests Money

Reads and Learns

Attention on the Future

Net Worth Driven

Thinks Big

Embraces Change

Compliments

Buys Time

Solves Problems

Multiple Flows of Income

Goal-Driven

11.1 **Overview**

Today, we're diving temporarily into the pit of despair known as the "Loser Mindset" – that swamp of stupidity, laziness and arrogance that has gobbled up people's opportunities to be wealthy. Well, gear up, because we're about to drop some wisdom bombs on the way and blast that loser mentality out of here like a cannonball from a pirate ship!

11.2 **Flock Followers**

Imagine a herd of sheep following the same old beaten path while the top 1% are out there carving a blazing trail where their money makes more money. Did you know the average poor and middle class persons have a safety-in-numbers mentality? They flock together and do what the others do. Research found that if you spend most of your time with five idiots, you will be the sixth. Likewise, if you spend your time with five millionaires, you will be the sixth. You are the average of the five people you spend the most time with. You listen to them, you think like them. You hear their words, you speak like them. You watch how they behave, you act like them. Psychologists call this "mirroring". Therefore, if they have no Kung Fu, you are likely to have none too.

11.3 Fear's Prisoners

Visualize being trapped in a horror movie marathon, terrified to even look at your own bank balance. Observe and you will notice that the poor and middle class are horrified of taking on risks because in their weak minds, risk equals loss. They are dead scared of losing money. If they have ever dabbled in investments, they buy high and sell low because of their flock mentality. Really? Yes really. Happens all the time.

Anyone fluent in the language of basic mathematics knows that when you buy high and sell low, you lose money! Why the fuck do people do that to themselves? Fear. Ignorance. Laziness. We will tackle the last two later.

Fear is an all-consuming emotion. When an asset price dips, and they see the crowd is flocking away from the market, they do the same – they sell low. This is fear escalating to panic. Trained investors call this market capitulation. This is why the poor and middle class remain poor and middle class. Lack of knowledge leads to fear. Fear leads to panic. Panic leads to the dark side.

After experiencing such losses, they typically never learn from their mistake, and they typically direct the blame towards others. They tend to never continue to invest. Any disposable money they have, they either choose to spend it or save it where it is "safe" – they put their money in the bank.

It has never occurred to the poor and middle class to think of what a bank does with their money. Banks never save the money they have in other banks! They fucking loan it out! They fucking buy bonds! They fucking invest! How else do you think banks are able to pay you a 3% time deposit interest if they do not invest your money to earn a bigger return? The poor spend. The middle class save. The rich invest. And banks are rich!

The poor and middle class, if they ever buy an investment asset, often recoil in terror the moment the price of that asset dips below the price they bought it at. Their balls shrink. Their throats go dry. They have no comprehension that price volatility is what produces life-changing returns. They fail to look at the asset's long-term price charts. Those wild swings between top and bottom, and then between bottom and new top, are what give you your life-changing returns. Volatility is your friend! Not your foe!

Those who operate on a low-level, poor people mindset are prone to take their money and run to the bank. These fucking losers feel "safe" earning a 3% annual interest, oblivious to the historical evidence that real inflation robs them of between10% to 20% of their purchasing power, compounded annually! Let's not even talk about the 100% CPI inflation witnessed in Argentina!

Losers think they are protecting their wealth by not losing money in the asset markets. The truth is they are protecting themselves from making money. This is self-sabotage. Getting fucked by governments, the elites and the banks is one thing. Fucking yourself like this is quite another thing.

11.4 **Ignorance is Bliss**

Think of wandering into a maze blindfolded and trying to find your way out. Ridiculous right? But this is what an alarming percentage of people do in the maze of life where retirement saving is crucial. In a report published in February of 2023, it was found that 42% of Americans have less than $1,000 in savings as of 2022.

Meanwhile a Standard & Poor's report found that worldwide, only 1 in 3 adults show an understanding of basic financial concepts. Alarmingly, it also found that billions of people are unprepared to deal with rapid changes in the financial landscape.

Financial literacy is found to have a direct correlation to wealth. A retirement crisis is said to be looming in Europe as governments slash public pensions and urge the population to work on their retirement planning. They are ill-prepared. The continent is plagued by chronic under-saving for old age.

In almost every country, statistics of retirement saving, or lack of it, point to how ignorant these Kung Fu-less people are. There is literally no excuse for this, given we live in the Age of Information.

Information is widely and densely available everywhere. The entire Internet is a vault of information, data, and knowledge across every conceivable subject matter. YouTube currently stands as the world's biggest social media platform with a staggering monthly active users number registered at over 3.5 billion users!

Yet, we are looking at only 60 million millionaires (denominated in US dollar) in the world, according to Visual Capitalist. It is safe to conclude that more than 99% of people on Earth are not clued in about how to build and preserve wealth.

This malaise can be attributed to our schooling system that broadly speaking teaches us nothing about money, central banks' fiat currency manufacturing, the necessity of creating multiple income streams, and the principles and practices of investing. Most people finish school and assume that their education has simultaneously come to a conclusion.

The inability to differentiate between schooling and education is a pandemic. Across the world, and especially in 3rd World countries, reading books to acquire life-changing knowledge is not on their to-do list at all. In the Age of Information, ignorance is a choice.

11.5 Lazy Complacency

These folks are like the couch potatoes of life, lounging around on their sofas and going through Netflix without any care for their own savings, investment and retirement planning. They simply possess no Kung Fu! Without Kung Fu, you can be easily killed. And without **Wealth Kung Fu**, you can be financially finished. What it all boils down to is laziness. Intellectual laziness is a disease because when left unchecked, it spreads. To us, this is already another pandemic.

Going by the shocking numbers on global financial literacy, 2 out of 3 people worldwide do not possess financial literacy. Ignorance is bliss. This is why the poor and middle class make up for the bottom 99%!

Be careful of your thoughts, WKF warrior. Lazy thoughts breed lazy words. Lazy words breed lazy habits. Lazy habits breed lazy characters. Lazy characters breed poor destinies.

We are acutely aware that the poor and the middle class work equally, if not more, hard than the rich. We are not talking about that. We are talking about the laziness of putting in the effort to learn and self-educate. Intellectual laziness is what we are referring to here.

In our research speaking with the poor, we were shocked to find out that an alarming number of them in a 3rd World country did not know how to do online banking even when they have attended high school, and were literate. They merely know how to withdraw their salaries from the ATM machine!

Asked why this was so, the replies were almost universally the same: we just don't know how to do online banking!

In a further research targeting Gen Xers in their 50s who have graduated with diplomas or degrees, we found that 3 out of every 5 while knowing how to do online banking, did not know how to do online shopping nor had any interest to learn!

Also 99% of these diploma and degree holders in their 50s only read traditional mainstream media news on and offline and had no correct knowledge of what Bitcoin really is! They continue to regurgitate that Bitcoin is a scam but could not explain why and how this cryptocurrency is a scam!

The year is 2023, man! The world's biggest asset manager, BlackRock, has filed for a Spot Bitcoin ETF. With all the information that's available, to still call bitcoin a scam has to be pretty darn stupid.

So, my dear wealth warrior, the question here is: whose fault is this? School has ended for these people, yes. Unfortunately, it looks like education has also ended for them! This kind of intellectual laziness must be the deep underlying cause on why they cannot escape the pit of the struggling class.

These respondents reeked of intellectual laziness. They just will not educate themselves in new technology or any new things. Their minds have shut down permanently, densely filled with cob-webs. These are minds that need to be unfucked.

11.6 **The Arrogance Veil**

This may be somewhat controversial, but to some observers, the poor and middle class have a veil of arrogance that is shielding them from seeing. One can say they are blinded by the Matrix. They see assets when the seeing see liabilities. They see risks when the seeing see opportunities. They see luck when the seeing see hard work. They see a world with too little money when the seeing see a world swimming in oceans of printed fiat currencies. What is it that's preventing the poor and middle class from seeing through the Matrix?

Answer: Arrogance.

Have you tried giving someone some free education about how Bitcoin has given annualized returns of roughly 145% between 2011 and middle of 2023? If you haven't, try it sometime. From our own experience, 9 in 10 will shrug it off and continue living with their habits and living in ignorance.

Only stupidity, laziness or arrogance can be the underlying cause. Maybe it's all three. The poor and middle class continue to be afflicted by this disease called arrogance. That's how they get poorer or stay mired in the pit of the middle class. Remember, financial literacy and wealth are directly correlated. Not having the Kung Fu to fight off your own financial illiteracy forever condemns you to the bottom-feeder rung.

Stupidity, intellectual laziness, and arrogance are a potent mix. It paralyzes the ability to learn, unlearn and relearn. It closes the door on new information and knowledge. It denies entry to facts, data and evidence. It shrouds the eyes from seeing any future projections. It blinds the mind from knowing a better future awaits. It numbs the body from feeling any positive vibrations and frequencies. It is a dangerous concoction.

The WKF master knows that this poisonous cup, when served, must quickly be high-kicked away! Expel any toxins of stupidity, intellectual laziness, and arrogance. Drink only from the cup of knowledge and let this rich tea wash down inside you as you reboost your energy and retune your frequencies to receive only positive charges to both mind and body. Ohmmm.

11.7 **The Negativity Paradox**

"I can never be like that."

"That's not for me."

"I don't know."

"This thing is for rich people, not me."

"Lucky fella. I don't have this sort of luck."

"Cannot."

Sounds familiar? These are simple words. But powerful words. They speak to those like peasants without Kung Fu skills. And so, their entire lives, they live like peasants too. It is a life choice. They allow anyone with Kung Fu to knock them down. And after that happens, they will continue to wallow in this self-pity. Nobody plays the victim card better than the poor!

Yes, the one who thinks he can and the one who thinks he can't, are both right. Poor people are constantly bugged down by negative thoughts. Negative thoughts breed negative words. Negative words breed negative actions (and inaction). Negative actions breed negative habits. Negative habits breed negative characters. Negative characters breed negative destinies.

No success, whether in business, in life, or in sports, can ever come out of a negative mindset. So, my WKF warrior, let this wisdom bomb always live in your mind. Negative people operate with a low-level, weak mentality. This kind of weak-ass mindset not only drags them down, it can drag you down too. The best thing to do when you come across negative people is to stay the fuck away from them!

11.8 Books Scorns

These are the folks rolling their eyes at books, like they're some sort of ancient torture device. Meanwhile, the rich devour books like they are ice cream on a scorching day.

Thomas Corley's study drops the mic: wealthy peeps read around 88 books a year. Books are wealthy people's secrets – they are gobbling up wisdom like there is no tomorrow.

We now live in an age where information has been made readily available everywhere. In fact, there is over-information. It's overloaded! If for whatever reason, a failing eye-sight for instance, you find reading books unpleasant, do not let this stop you from building up on your WKF knowledge, for fuck's sake! Don't be lazy!

There is always YouTube, considered by some to be the world's biggest library. Over 30 million channels exist in this digital ecosystem. Experts readily make videos and educate everyone for free! You can learn almost anything! So why don't you?

Perhaps the secret to having a life of abundance is in this mantra: **Schooling ends. Education doesn't.**

Every **Wealth Kung Fu** warrior must let this mantra be their guiding light.

11.9 **Vanity Parade**

Imagine strutting around like a peacock but your bank account is flatter than a pancake. Bankrate's got the scoop: nearly 30% of adults have more credit card debt than savings.

The poor and middle class, whenever they have access to money, like to show-off. Wearing an expensive t-shirt with a huge designer logo emblazoned in front is their thing. They also buy shoes, watches, cars and houses they can ill-afford. This is risky behaviour. They are trying to show the world they are rich. But the discerning can see the Emperor has no clothes!

The poor and middle class use credit to buy shit. And almost all of them do this while simultaneously building up debt! Eeks!

On the other hand, the rich do buy luxury items but without credit. Typically, they buy such liabilities (we explained this pretty thoroughly in Volume 1) from the passive income streams generated by assets they own.

This is completely opposite to the liabilities bought by the poor and middle class. Those are bought with salaries, money they worked for.

There is a whole world of difference between the WKF master who owns a new BMW paid for by the dividends from his business, or shares he owns, or rentals he received (all generated by his assets), and the WKF-less peacock who owns a new BMW paid for by her monthly salary, which she had to earn by trading her time and energy for.

Okay, comrade, our mission isn't just to roast the losers – it's to turn you into an investing hero! Let's kick that loser mindset to the curb, grab the champion mentality by the horns, and conquer the investment world like a boss! Avoid that loser mindset and adopt that rich mindset, if you haven't already. If you don't imagine yourself having abundance, you will never get started. Unfucking that loser mindset is not an option if you want to be successful.

Chapter 12:

Unfucking That Loser Mindset

Alright, you badass warrior, strap in because we're about to unfuck any remnants of that loser mindset you might still be harbouring in the deeper recesses of your mind. In other words, here are the lessons for you to relearn and absorb the tao of wisdom known as the "Winner Mindset" – a **Wealth Kung Fu** powerhouse that is as kickass as a Kung Fu master knocking out 33 baddies in one fight!

The Winner Mindset is your golden scroll to learn and to become a true **Wealth Kung Fu** master.

12.1 The Rich Never Stop Learning

You will find the rich have one thing in common – the penchant for continuous learning. As beautifully as the water flows from the stream to the river, and from the river to the sea, so must the flow of knowledge travel into the mind of the **Wealth Kung Fu** master.

The poor and middle class think schooling and education are the same thing. That is why they remain poor and middle class. Schools, being part of the diabolical Matrix

Being **broke** is hard.

Being **wealthy** is hard.

CHOOSE
your hard.

to chain people to slavery, have never taught any pupil about building wealth. And so, 99% of people remain mired in the mosh pit of either poverty or middle class misery. For the poor, that is hell. For the middle class, that is like being stuck in Purgatory forever!

Those with the iron Kung Fu will to succeed have always pushed themselves into learning new things. Because they know - schooling and education are two different things. Schooling stops. Education does not.

The ability to unlearn, learn and relearn is especially important in this rapidly changing financial landscape. The moment you accept this and start changing your behaviour on this, your life will start to pivot. And so shall your destiny, my friend. Get your muscular hands on all the wealth-building books, blogs, and videos that you can. The more you learn, the more you will unlearn and relearn. Reading books and watching videos that provide financial education gives you an endless flowing Chi of financial literacy that will feed your head and energise your will to succeed.

12.2 The Rich Have A Superpower Called Delayed Gratification

Delayed Gratification. That's some fucking Kung Fu, man! It is a superpower absent in a lot of people including second and third generation millionaires and billionaires! That is why family fortunes seldom last beyond two generations!

99% of motherfuckers, when rained with cash, inevitably blow that cash away like a lottery winner on a shopping orgy! What would you do if you were to inherit $100 million today? Will you buy that dream beach-front mansion and that sexy Ferrari? Or will you delay instant gratification and invest that $100 million for a 10x return? A 10x return means you will then have a cool billion! Few have such willpower.

Remember, my WKF Tiger Claw champ, the fighter who can defeat the enemies within becomes a truly dangerous person. The enemies without will stand no chance.

Delayed gratification is a discipline. Saving is a discipline. Investing is a discipline. Reinvesting your capital plus your gains is a discipline. Discipline is a superpower. It is the result of a person with absolute mental toughness. It separates the successful from the unsuccessful, the rich from the poor.

There is no Kung Fu without discipline. And without Kung Fu, you're very killable. Same goes for **Wealth Kung Fu**.

12.3 The Rich Work Their Asses Off

People judge the successful by the results they show. But almost none of these people know what it took to get there. The losers attribute such success to luck. This is why they are always broke. They do not see behind the veil of success that successful people put in a lot of time, capital and effort to produce the result they dreamed of. Don't be fooled by the old couple lounging lazily by the poolside of a swanky, 5-star resort, wearing their Rolex Daytona and Patek Philippe Aquanaut wristwatches. These two have earned it many times over. Look harder and you will find that there is at least one book, magazine or digital tablet by their side.

If you actually have the courage to approach them and speak to them, you will likely find out that these two, typical of the rich, have put in a lot of time and effort into making their fortune.

85% of such people did not inherit wealth. They built it from zero! Believe us when we say to you: 85% of rich people put in a lot of hard work to get to where they are. Sure, there was knowledge. Sure, there were savings. Sure, there was help from others (i.e. network). But there was a lot of hard work. Pain. Suffering. Humiliation, perhaps. This kind of workhorse ethics is what has seen the poor and the middle class flipped their destinies from the have-nots to the haves.

So if one day, a friend surprises you by driving up in a brand new Porsche, don't think he's lucky. Think what kind of shit he had to go through to be able to afford one now. Ask him the questions behind his success. Ask him about his work ethics! It's the question unsuccessful people do not ask! You will be surprised what the answer is. You will be surprised to learn his work-ethics, his ability to work hard, work smart and work longer in spite of the whiplashes he had to take, far outweigh and out-distance yours! No pain, no gain. This is some **Wealth Kung Fu**!

12.4 The Rich Do Not Follow The Herd

Winners don't follow the herd. If you do, you will be in the bottom 99%. Whenever you are surrounded by people who talk about other people, news events and other such bullshit with no modicum of intelligence or substance, it is time to walk away.

Even when you come across someone well educated but is argumentative and talks only to hear his own voice, or always tries to ram his viewpoints down your throat in the hope you will agree with him, zip up. Say as little as possible. Conserve your positive Chi for other people who deserve your time and energy. Egotistical people have a big chip on their shoulders and are very toxic. You don't have to expand any energy crossing swords with them. And you don't have to share anything you know with them. They simply do not listen.

Reassess your circle of friends and contacts. When you do, you will see the need to either discard or shrink it. Go with those who have ambition, vision, and positive Chi. The truly wealthy and successful tend to listen very carefully when you speak. They are assessing whether you are a liability or an asset to them! Should they find your company beneficial, rest assured you will be welcomed to the next gathering where other such high value friends of theirs will also meet you. This is one of the key reasons why the successful keep getting more successful. They know how to build a network that builds their net worth!

So, my dear warrior, surely you must remember the image of the lone Kung Fu master? He walks alone. When he is not alone, he is teaching his students. When he is with his friends, this is usually at a table with other masters. When he is at a fight, he fights alone. And he fights the baddest!

It is ok to be a misanthrope. Often in the investment arena, your contrarian moves against the flow of the crowd shall bring seismic returns. This is ultimately what separates the top 1% from the bottom 99%. Our rebellion is against the Matrix, the elites, and the unthinking herd who follows it.

12.5 The Rich Take Risks To Build Wealth

Winners don't play it safe all the damn time. They know when to throw down some chips and take bets. Not taking the risk to own some Bitcoin, for example, has been said to be the biggest risk of all for an investor today. Should the market capitalization of Bitcoin grow from $500 billion to $10 trillion in the future, not having at least a 1% allocation to Bitcoin would result in missing out on a 20x or 2,000% gain. This is why even the world's biggest asset management institution, BlackRock, has in 2023 put in an application to the SEC (Securities Exchange Commission) for a spot Bitcoin ETF. Not getting off zero in Bitcoin is too big a risk even for BlackRock!

Data show that 1990s and early 2000s investors who were afraid to allocate some of their capital into tech stocks like Google, Microsoft, Apple, Amazon and Facebook missed out on making some of the biggest gains in the history of the stock market of the last 30 years. They failed to understand that these highly volatile stocks, with their high risk-reward ratio and violent short term price swings, are the assets that would bring staggering, life-changing returns. When you scrutinize these brand names now, you know that it would have taken a lot of market research, a visionary mind and investment gumption in those early days to pick these stocks. Those few who did must now be relating their legendary forays to their families and friends on their private yachts, one imagines.

In contrast, the middle class like to play it "safe" and park their money in banks, blue-chip stocks, and bonds, all of which typically produce single digit returns. The interest rates of bank deposits that yield 0.1% to 3% per year are always deemed "safe" by the financially illiterate. Safe from what? You can always see your capital preserved there plus a few dollars added yearly in interest, but your purchasing power is eroding like a motherfucker at a far higher compounded rate!

This lack of intelligence is the result of the Matrix's heavily manipulated school curriculum, which did not teach us about how banks really work and how inflation actually steals our wealth, and how the fiat Ponzi (something we will go into detail on in our forthcoming Volume 3) has enslaved the world population since 1971.

If you are not a risk-taker, you will never build wealth. If you never build wealth, you will always remain poor or broke. The fiat Ponzi and the Matrix have been built to see to that!

Protecting yourself from losing money in the markets is actually protecting yourself from making money. This is a dumbass move. This is self-sabotage at its worst. Who the fuck grows wealth from mere savings? Inflation will knock you out, you dumbass! Inflation is the nefarious badass that finishes off people without **Wealth Kung Fu**!

So, my WKF comrade, unfuck your own mind if you know you are harbouring any laziness, lack of knowledge, fear of investment risks or indiscipline. Kick that bullshit to the curb, and let your brilliance shine brighter than a supernova partying at a cosmic rave!

Chapter 13:

WTF Are Assets?

Great acts
are made up of
small deeds

— Lao Tze —

13.1 **WTF are Assets?**

Hey there, my dear WKF warrior, ready to throw down some Kung Fu moves on your money matters? Let's deep dive into the world of investment assets. Think of this like cracking open a treasure chest in a hidden kingdom – except the treasure is knowledge, and the kingdom is your wealth destination. So, gear up, because we're about to lay down the wisdom bombs that shall have you navigating the treacherous terrains of the investment world with the calmness of a Zen master.

An asset is a store of value item (both physical and digital, we must add) that puts money in your pocket. It's as simple as that! Over time, an asset grows in value; Wall Street calls this "capital gain". As such, owning an asset fundamentally sends your money to work for you. Think of it as sending your army to capture more army.

But hold up, there's more! These investment assets aren't just flashy moves for show. They are the unsung heroes that keep hustling while you are busy doing other stuff, or nothing at all. It's like having your money do push-ups when you are not looking!

Just like a Kung Fu master growing their strength day after day, these assets grow over time, compounding your wealth slowly but surely. Now, here's the kicker: Google shares on 6 August 2011 was $12. Twelve years later, on 11 August 2023, it was $177. This was a cumulative gain of 1,475%! That's one powerful Kung Fu flying kick that instantly knocks down your old nemesis, Inflation, and send it into comatose oblivion! Hee-yahhh! Boom!

Liabilities, conversely, takes money out of your pocket. Again, it's as simple as that. A house you live in, for example, is a liability. Why? Because it takes money out of your pocket. I know, I know... the house is likely to give you capital gain as its price is likely to inch up year by year. But let us tai chi back to you this: if this is your only home, will you sell it? If the answer is no, then the house that you live in is by definition a liability.

So, in the Kung Fu of building wealth and protecting wealth, do this one thing for the rest of your life - buy assets. Own as many as you can. The poor buy liabilities thinking they are assets. The rich minimise buying liabilities and add on to their assets.

Remember the lesson from **Wealth Kung Fu Vol 1**? Assets minus liabilities define your Net Worth! The poor and middle class tend to focus on income. The rich focus on net worth. These two kicks are different. The first one is weak and has little impact on your opponent – inflation. The second is powerful and can KO your inflation opponent down instantly. Kapow! Yippy-ka-yay, motherfucker!

A word about

Liabilities

Let's talk about the other pesky villain in this story –
liabilities.

These sneaky troublemakers are like the banana peels
of your **Wealth Kung Fu** journey. Think loans, credit card
debt, unsettled bills and other financial boogeymen.
They're the party crashers to your WKF shindig. But don't
fret, my Preying Mantis – roundhouse kick every single
one of these motherfuckers one at a time.

Before you know it, these fuckers lie dead at your feet.
Now step over them and continue your heroic journey
debt-free. Remember, without debt and liabilities, you
now have a positive net worth. The only risks you need
to take are calculated ones on each asset that you have
decided to buy.

IF YOUR
SALARY
IS YOUR ONLY
SOURCE OF
INCOME,
YOU ARE
ONE STEP
AWAY FROM
POVERTY.

Do not, for fuck's sake, take the advice from some gurus to build wealth by taking on debt! Investing on borrowed money is the fastest way to financial ruins. A market downturn, which always happens, will see your property become tenantless. A stock market dip will send your leveraged shares into forced selling aka liquidation. Both can kick you falling into the chasm of insolvency faster than you can say, Robert Kiyosaki. Bankruptcies that come from these high-risk plays are fairly common. Best leave the dark arts of taking on long-term debt and stock market leveraging to the professionals.

Your long-term journey is paved with sound sleepful nights when you have no debt and no liabilities. Trust us. This is a very nice place to be!

Alright, warrior of wealth! Investment assets are like your ultimate weaponry, guiding you to victory in the fight for wealth. They are not just numbers on paper. So, embrace these investment assets like a Kung Fu maestro embracing their inner zen.

The journey is just as exhilarating as the destination, my friend. Let your assets be the rockstars of your WKF adventure, choreographing a tale of triumph that maybe, will be talked about for generations.

13.2 Why Assets Make You Rich

Listen up, you magnificent money warrior, because it's time to uncover the damn wizardry behind assets that can make you roll in the money dough. Get your wits ready for this mind-bending journey into the realm of why assets are the fucking secret sauce to becoming a bona fide WKF maestro.

Assets as Turbo Boosters

Alright, buckle up, daredevil, because we're about to turbocharge your game. Assets? Yeah, they're like strapping a damn jetpack on your money and launching it to the wealth stratosphere faster than a Kung Fu master's lightning punch!

1. The Symphony of Passive Income:
Imagine assets as backstage passes to the
concert of ka-ching! Real estate's the headliner
here, belting out an average annual return
of 6.4% from 2000 to 2019, according to the
National Association of Real Estate Investment
Trusts (NAREIT). That's like owning a VIP ticket
that not only gets you into the show but showers
you with groupies too!

2. The Mind-Boggling Magic of Appreciation: Just
like a Kung Fu sensei refining their chops, assets
like stocks have their own damn magic show.
Apart from the 1,475% appreciation of the Google
share price we highlighted earlier, there are other
assets known to have given its owner the coveted
10x return, something we highlighted extensively
in **Wealth Kung Fu Vol 1**. The trick is to find them.

In 1998, Amazon's share price opened at $0.24. By 11 August 2023, 25 years later, its share price closed at $138! This is a 57,512% ROI (Return On Investment) or a 575x move!

The question is: do you have the smarts to pick the next asset like Amazon or Apple? Not impossible if you put in enough work on studying assets. And after you have done so, do you have the gumption to ride it up and down over a long period of time without selling it? Easy, if you know you hold a truly sound asset.

Finally, do you have the Zen-like calm of a Shaolin temple monk and sell it during a market high to lock in your profit without ever succumbing to the what-if greed of waiting for another all-time-high? Difficult but this is what a WKF master does. They know the mantra – **No one ever goes broke locking in profits by selling!**

3. The Inflation-Defying Battle:

Assets are your ultimate "Take that, inflation!" roundhouse kick. They put your biggest enemy, Inflation, in a headlock and teach it some damn manners!

So, you hard-muscled daredevil, wrap your head around this – assets are your not-so-secret weapons in the battle for wealth supremacy. These bad boys aren't just hanging around. They are your partners-in-profit, knocking down financial challenges that stand in your way, and charging forward like your own personal army to reach freedom land.

As you master the art of asset domination, you are not just stacking up – you are crafting an epic saga of WKF awesomeness that will echo through the ages. You are making this saga yours. You are making yourself the main character in this saga! Fuck, yeah!

13.3 Go from White Belt to Black Belt in Asset Accumulation

Alright, hero, fasten your investment belt because we're about to take you from white belt to black belt. Imagine this journey as an adrenaline-pumping Kung Fu saga, filled with twists, turns, and the ultimate goal of mastering the art of accumulating wealth.

Step 1

Grasp the Fundamentals - Your WKF Stance

Just as a Kung Fu master perfects their stances, you need to master the fundamentals of each investment assets. Each asset like a building, a stock, gold, silver, bitcoin, Ethereum, XRP and even a Patek Philippe, has its own inherent fundamentals. Study them and find out what has made it so desirable and what kind of demand will it create in the foreseeable future. Study its market or industry forces. What do the market cycle charts over the last few decades tell you? How long does its cycle high averages? How long does its cycle low averages? Cross-reference these cycle ups and downs with macro-economic data. Did the lows coincide with an economic recession? Did the highs coincide with an economic boom? Most likely, history shall either rhyme or repeat itself. Your entry and exit points are already determined for you once you plough through these data!

Embrace the Discipline of Consistency - Your Daily Kung Fu Practice

Similar to the discipline of a martial artist's daily practice, your investment journey thrives on consistent efforts. Research reveals that investors who consistently put in the work over time achieve superior results compared to those lazy fucks who do little to no work in researching and only have sporadic engagements to show. DYOR (Do Your Own Research) over and over again. Not just in buying or selling but in monitoring your assets and their market developments as you hold them. This is akin to honing your Kung Fu skills through persistent practice.

Step 3

Reside in the Magic of Compounding

Ah, the mystical power of compound interest – it's your secret recipe for success, much like a hidden Kung Fu technique. Nurturing your investments over time by basically doing fuck all (i.e. not selling until they reach their price targets that you have set before you bought them) is the awesomeness of a Zen master.

The stock market is strewn with examples of ten-baggers or 10 Xers (lengthily explained in Volume 1) that have given their owners at least a 1,000% return over time. If you take inflation at 10%, all these sound assets have given an ROI of over 10% per year, effectively kicking inflation in the teeth year after year.

One stellar example is Bitcoin, the King of cryptocurrency. By August 2023, about 14 years after inception, at a price of $30,000 per bitcoin, this asset has produced an annualized return of 149%!

Step 4
Diversify Your Arsenal

As you progress, the art of diversification becomes your core strategy – envision it as the adaptability of a Kung Fu master. Historical performance data underscore the significance of spreading your investments across varied asset classes. This strategy acts as a shield against market volatility, fortifying your assets stronghold.

Step 5
Craft Your Investment Kata

Just as a Kung Fu hero creates their unique sequence of moves, craft your investment kata – a tailored strategy aligned with your aspirations. Analyze historical data like a professor, studying all strengths, weaknesses, threats and opportunities... also known as SWOT analysis. This empowers you to execute astute investment moves and sidestep risks. Remember, in more ways than one, investing is about taking on risks but managing those risks as best as you can.

Step 6
Seek Wisdom from Senseis

Just as a Kung Fu disciple learns from wise mentors, so too must you. Seek insights from seasoned investment experts. Our experience tells us that engaging with investment mentors and continually educating yourself about investment principles, rules and practices often lead to superior outcomes. This is akin to receiving invaluable guidance from a venerable Kung Fu elder, your Sifu.

Step 7
Stay Agile and Alert

Flexibility serves as your armour in the investment arena, similar to a Kung Fu master's agility against ever-changing opponents. Historical market data emphasize the importance of remaining nimble. In the age of digital technology and fast-moving digital media, swift adaptation to market shifts and capitalizing on strategic opportunities can substantially influence the success of your investment journey.

So, my valiant one, as you ascend from a novice to donning the revered black belt of asset accumulation, remember that this expedition demands unwavering dedication, unwavering discipline, and an insatiable thirst for information empowerment.

Moreover, the S&P 500, a prominent stock market index, has displayed an average annual growth rate of around 10% over several decades, exemplifying the potential for appreciation within the realm of stocks.

The phenomenon of compound interest, observed over numerous investment timelines, reveals that even modest investments with an average annual interest rate of 10% can lead to significant accumulation over time. For example, with a capital of $10,000 and an annual compounding rate of 10%, you will have $67,275 after 20 years.

Chapter 14

Modern Investment Assets

14.1 Cryptocurrencies

Hey there, you bold investment adventurer! Buckle up for a wild ride through the LED-lit realm of modern investment assets – and guess who's stealing the spotlight? Yup, you got it – the phenomenal Cryptocurrencies! These digital marvels are like the martial arts master's weapons of the investing world – quick, powerful, and ready to flip things upside down.

Hold onto your hat, because we're diving headfirst into the crypto-verse, where every cryptocurrency is like a character with their own killer moves. Leading the parade of financial rockstars is none other than the legend himself, Bitcoin. This dude's a straight-up titan in the crypto-verse, commanding respect and attention from every corner of the investment playground.

But wait, let's sprinkle in some real-world stats to throw the spotlight on this electrifying story. Bitcoin's market cap skyrocketing from zero in 2009 to a jaw-dropping $1 trillion mark in 2021 – that was like a mic drop moment heard around the world of finance!

Now, shift your gaze to Ethereum, the quicksilver sorcerer, flaunting a market cap that has soared beyond $300 billion – a badge of honour in the mystical realm of smart contracts and decentralized magic.

Now, imagine Ripple XRP as the slick and fluid ninja of the bunch, gliding through the financial currents with transaction speeds that leave traditional bank settlement systems choking on their dust. And hey, here comes Litecoin, the agile sidekick to Bitcoin's superhero – often called the "silver" to Bitcoin's "gold," it's like watching a martial arts pro showing off their killer dance moves.

But hold your horses, we're not done yet! Behold the Solana coin, the faster-than-Ethereum of the cryptocurrency realm, doing its thing to fuel the fiery core of digital assets exchanges, with its market value shooting past $80 billion like a rocket.

But in the midst of this flashy show, don't forget about the sneaky stuff – the crypto realm's got its own share of tricksters and shady characters, like a bunch of mischievous ninjas ready to mess with your game. Yes, there are nefarious characters in this nascent space. But fear not, because with enough knowledge and a dash of **Wealth Kung Fu** instinct, you can be better prepared to enter this arena and navigate your way to your final 10x destination. Prior to the 2022 cryptocurrency crash, when coins hit new all time highs, not only was a 10x move from their previous bottom a regularity, but a 100x move was not uncommon in the smaller, riskier coins!

Cryptocurrencies can produce returns that are dazzling, but hold your horses – their wild swings can rival a hyperactive martial arts newbie on a sugar high. So, my daring disciple, keep your balance, choose your crypto carefully, and ride these market waves like a rodeo cowboy.

And here's the lowdown – diversification is your secret weapon! We expanded on this strategy in Volume 1 and if you've read it, you'd know diversification of your portfolio is the hallmark of every wealthy Kung Fu master.

Just like a martial arts hotshot who's got a bunch of moves up their sleeve, spreading your investments across a range of assets shields you from the shock of a single flop.

So, there you have it, cryptocurrencies emerging like majestic dragons in the digital sky is a fantastic sight to behold – untamed, fierce, and oh-so-impressive. Those daredevils who joined the fray during its early inception years have become multimillionaires in less than a decade! A 10,000x return, something quite unheard of in other asset classes, was not a myth. It did happen!

But beware, my WKF master. This is a stage filled with nefarious actors, people with bad intentions. Not every coin has sound fundamentals. Most do not even have a use-case. At the time of writing, it has been reported that over 20,000 coins exist. Many cryptocurrency observers have publicly declared 99% of these coins would go to zero. Meme coins, created as internet jokes or as satirical send-offs, are especially risky! Do not touch them with the proverbial 10-foot pole!

14.2 **Bitcoin**

Well, well, well, buckle up, you adventurous WKF daredevil, because we're about to deep-dive into the wild world of the King of all cryptocurrencies – Bitcoin!

Imagine a digital revolution that flips the finger to traditional finance – that's Bitcoin for ya! This cryptocurrency burst onto the scene in 2009 like a rockstar crashing a boring party, and it's been making heads spin ever since. While traditional money bows down to governments and banks, Bitcoin's like that renegade martial artist who doesn't give a shit about authority.

Created by a person or persons unknown, Bitcoin's genesis came from the pseudonymous Satoshi Nakamoto in 2008 with their release of the Bitcoin White Paper entitled, **Bitcoin: A Peer-to-Peer Electronic Cash System**. This all-important, eight-page white paper is widely available on the Internet and is a must-read for everyone interested in Bitcoin. We highly recommend you read it!

Bitcoin Characteristics:

- *A software protocol built on a Blockchain.*

- *Capped supply of 21 million coins.*

- *Secured by Cryptography and Maths.*

- *Decentralized.*

- *Transparent.*

- *Open Sourced.*

- *Private.*

- *Permissionless.*

- *Divisible.*

- *Fungible.*

- *Portable.*

- *Deflationary.*

Now let's glance at some numbers. Back in 2010, Bitcoin was worth less than your grandma's spare change – we're talking a measly $0.003! Fast forward to today in August 2023, and you might just drop your coffee when you realize a single Bitcoin is now at $30,000! That's a 1,000,000,000% return! That's not a run-away train. That's a rocket!

But here's the real game-changer – Bitcoin isn't just about the Benjamins, honey. It's about toppling the old-school financial system, giving a big middle finger to Central Banks and their fiat currencies, something we will go into great details on in an upcoming **Bitcoin** book. Wait for it!

For now, the important thing to digest is, unlike your regular cash, Bitcoin isn't printed to infinity out of thin air by some dude in a suit. There is a limited supply – only 21 million Bitcoin will ever be mined. This is a genius move that guarantees your Bitcoin stack will not be be diluted into shitty fiat currencies mush!

Now, a word about Blockchain technology. This is quite the fancy-pants technology that resides on the Internet. It keeps tabs on every single Bitcoin move. It's like a Kung Fu sensei's watchful eye, making sure there's no monkey business. Every transaction, every in and out in this digital open ledger is observable. Transparency, security, and authenticity – the blockchain has got them all covered. No more shady accounting bullshit or shifty tricks – it's all out in the open.

But hold onto your hats because here comes the caution – Bitcoin's got mood swings that put hormonal teenagers to shame. In a single day, it can shoot up like a rocket or crash down like a failed high kick in high heels. That's why, my fearless Panda, when you dive into Bitcoin, channel your inner Kung Fu Zen master. Stay chill and keep your Kung Fu calm and strong.

So, as you waltz into the mesmerizing world of Bitcoin, remember this is not just any cryptocurrency – it's a revolution against the norm, a middle finger to money printing and manipulation. Whether you're a crypto noob or a seasoned investor-warrior, embracing Bitcoin is like strapping on the armour of a WKF gladiator. This is a major investment asset that has the potential to take over the planet as a global reserve currency!

More will be unravelled in our next Volume on **Bitcoin**!

Meanwhile, here is a Bitcoin chart for you to mull over:

BITCOIN RETURNS: 2010 – 2023

Year	Year Start	Year End	% Change
2010	0.003	0.30	9,900%
2011	0.30	4.72	1,473%
2012	4.72	13.5	186%
2013	13.5	758	5,507%
2014	758	320	-58%
2015	320	430	35%
2016	430	968	125%
2017	968	13,860	1,331%
2018	13,860	3,689	-73%
2019	3,689	7,184	95%
2020	7,184	28,775	301%
2021	28,775	47,902	66%
2022	47,902	16,531	-65%
2023 YTD 17.09.23	16,531	26,560	61%

At this point of writing, the Bitcoin annualized return since 2011 is 149%. Is this the super-asset of our time? Given this sort of CAGR (Compounded Annual Growth Rate), it seems this is the Holy Grail of all investment assets. A 10x or 1000% return has happened over and over again throughout Bitcoin's history and in far greater quantum than any traditional investor could have hoped for! Is it any wonder then, that investors who have discovered and studied Bitcoin are barely looking at anything else?

Once again, it bears reminding that we are not here to give financial advice. We are merely providing facts, information and findings, sometimes peppered with our personal opinion, none of which you should take as investment advice. Ultimately, you must learn all the risks and consult a professional if necessary. Any and all investment decisions are yours to make and yours only.

That said, we shall go on to inform you that Bitcoin adoption based on the current available wallets and addresses have numbered no more than 1.5% of the global population of 8 billion people. The current Bitcoin market capitalization is hovering at $500 billion approximately.

Compared to gold's market cap of $11 trillion, do you know how many Xs Bitcoin can move up by in order for it to equal gold's market cap? 20x! At the present price of $26,000 per Bitcoin, a 20x move will take the price of Bitcoin to $520,000 per coin. It seems astonishing and improbable, but maths doesn't lie!

This is the sort of investor wet dream that we are all lucky to be living in right now. What happens when the next 3% of the human population wakes up to this reality and starts adopting Bitcoin? What happens when the next 5% does? The mind boggles.

This is why it is not uncommon for Bitcoiners to publicly predict a $1 million to $10 million Bitcoin! These figures are far from preposterous once you've worked out the maths of how a finite supply of 21 million coins gets superboosted in price against a dysfunctional fiat monetary system that is collapsing in slow motion!

Clearly, this subject deserves an entire **Wealth Kung Fu** book on its own! Wait for it!

14.3 Alternative Assets

Well, buckle up as we plunge headfirst into the wonderfully bizarre realm of alternative assets – the investment world's version of a psychedelic trip that'll have you rethinking those boring-ass stocks and bond shenanigans! These mysterious tooth-fairies are like the little-known treasures of the hidden investment cave that 99% of people are not aware of.

Now, imagine this – while the masses are playing it "safe" in the traditional investment playground of real estate, bonds, and equities, it's the millionaire cool cats who are tossing alternative assets around like a pro juggler!

Now turn your attention to some alternative assets because here comes the plot twist fine wine and rare whisky! These aren't just beverages for snobs, they are like the James Bond gadgets of the investment realm. Some esoteric whisky bottles have seen gains of over 500% in just a few years. It's like sipping your way to a jackpot! Without naming the brand, we know of vintage years wine bottles that have given a 1,000% or 10x return to their buyers!

But hang tight, my brave soul, and let us take you down another whacky trail in the mysterious world of alternative assets – relics of the past. We personally know an accountant who has three dinosaur eggs in his safekeeping. These eggs were dug out from the deep soils of China and he paid a considerable sum for the dino eggs about a decade ago. He has so far turned down offers that would have given him a 1,000% return. He reckons these eggs should cost more. Maybe you're hearing the X-Files theme in your head right now? Who can blame you? The rich can be eccentric and funny in their own way.

These alternative assets aren't for the faint-hearted or the couch potatoes. They demand a dash of audacity, for the wonderfully scarce. After all, you can say all assets only have values based on their investors' bias and perception, What is gold if not just a shiny rock? Is Mona Lisa really worth $100,000,000?

In the glittering world of luxury watches, three holy trinity of brands have quite recently come to be acknowledged by the financial world as assets – Rolex, Patek Philippe, and Audemars Piguet.

Ever since a pronounced spike in demand in 2018, Rolex sports models have seen their after market price increased two to three folds. A stainless steel Rolex Cosmograph Daytona is retailed in a Rolex authorised dealer for $15,100 in 2023. But because demand is so overwhelmingly high, you cannot find a displayed piece for sale. They only display "for exhibition" pieces. The waiting list is rumoured to be 20 years!

The only practical way you can purchase such a watch now is in the grey market. Chronos 24, an online after-market watch platform, has a brand new stainless steel Rolex Cosmograph Daytona listed for $36,000. This is the price of scarcity. No wonder institutions such as Goldman Sachs has classified such watches as "assets". Don't even get us started on the Patek Philippe Nautilus!

We personally know of a multimillionaire whose Rolex and Patek Philippe collection constitutes 100% of his investment portfolio! Real estate, stocks, gold and cryptocurrencies do not turn him on!

For relatively more "grounded" investors like you and I, mixing up our portfolios with alternative assets can inject some spice, adding a dash of colour and a pinch of thrill in this **Wealth Kung Fu** journey.

So, my risk-taking rebel, take the plunge into the world of alternative assets but not before you know what you are doing. Embrace the odd, the wild, and the zany, if you must. Let these unconventional investments be your additional secret weapons to battle that behemoth of baddies - Inflation. Just remember, while the rest are stuck in snoozeland, you'll be out there busting moves and turning your investment journey into one hell of a kickass saga. Kapow!

Chapter 15:

Investing

15.1 WTF is Investing?

Hey, you Dragon master! Buckle up, because we're about to take a wild ride into the world of investing – the ultimate money Kung Fu! Think of it as flexing your financial muscles and making your cash do some serious heavy lifting. So, grab your money nunchucks, let's dive in, and demystify this investing shit.

Alright, let's strip away the financial mumbo-jumbo and get to the real deal. Investing is like planting money seeds with the hope they'll grow into money trees that drop cash instead of leaves. We're not talking about throwing your money around like confetti at a lame party; we're talking about calculated moves. Picture this: you're buying into companies, dipping your toes into real estate waters, riding the rollercoaster of cryptocurrencies, or even being a part of a startup adventure. It's not just a money toss – it's a strategic money placement for maximum growth.

But hold on, hotshot! Investing isn't some magic shortcut to becoming an overnight millionaire. This isn't a fairy tale where you find a money beanstalk, it's more like training in a dojo. You start as a rookie, learn the moves, and level up over time. It's about strategy, persistence, and keeping an open mind.

Wrap your head around this: investing is like having an army of financial warriors working for you while you chill on a beach sipping cocktails. It's like the ultimate Kung Fu combo that keeps on giving. You put in the effort, set your plan, and let the magic of compounding do its thing. It's the kind of move that knocks out financial opponents without breaking a sweat.

But don't be fooled. The investment dojo isn't all Zen and meditation; it's more like a rowdy brawl with market curveballs that can smack you in the face. But here's the kicker: knowledge and preparation are your Kung Fu weapons. Armed with these, you can dodge financial punches and counter like a pro fighter, leaving your opponents scratching their heads.

Now, let's flash some numbers for a sec. Over the years, the stock market has averaged around 7-10% annual returns. I know it might not sound as flashy as a Bruce Lee move, but it adds up. Imagine this: you invest $5,000 now; at a 7% annual return, you'd be sitting on over $38,000 in 30 years. Now that's some legit financial Kung Fu action!

So, fellow money master, let's gear up and dive into the world of investing – the ultimate money martial art. Educate yourself, practice your moves, and step into the financial ring with the swagger of a seasoned Kung Fu warrior. Remember, this isn't a sprint; it's a money marathon, just like mastering Kung Fu. So go ahead, grab your financial katana, strike your wealth-building pose, and let's conquer the investment world like the badasses we are! Ka-Ching!

15.2 Five Strategies Used in Investing

Greetings, astute seeker of financial enlightenment! As we continue our expedition into the intricate realm of investing, I shall unveil before you the five strategic pillars wielded by battle-hardened investors - a repertoire akin to a Kung Fu grandmaster's diverse techniques. Each manoeuvre, is a potent tool in your arsenal, mirroring the adaptability of a seasoned martial artist adjusting to different opponents. So, gather around as I illuminate the essence of these five investment Kung Fu techniques, interwoven with real-world insights and tangible data.

1. Value Investing - The Discount Hunter.

Picture this: you're at a garage sale, spotting the hidden gems among the junk. That's value investing, my amigo. You're on the hunt for stocks that are practically yelling "buy me, buy me!" Warren Buffett is the master here - turning Berkshire Hathaway from a $18 puppy to a $419,315 beast per share. That's like Bruce Lee levelling up to dragon status!

2. Growth Investing - High-Speed Money Chase.

Ever seen a cheetah chasing prey? That's growth investing, baby! You're after those companies that are sprinting to success. It's like spotting your buddy's weak point in a nerf gun fight and nailing it. Amazon? They went from selling books to ruling the world. Their stock? From $18 to over $186. Growth investors are like adrenaline junkies, seeking that financial thrill ride.

3. Income Investing - Cha-Ching Cash Dance.

Imagine your money throwing a cash party. That's income investing, folks. It's all about getting those regular money drops. Dividend stocks, rentals, and bonds are your crew, protecting you like bodyguards. Rentals in the US? 5% to 10% annual return. And dividends? It's like having your money sing you a sweet lullaby.

4. Index Investing - Chill Zen Monk Mode.

Index investing is your financial Zen mode. You're chill like a Kung Fu master in meditation while chaos rages around you. It's like finding your centre and holding that Kung Fu pose. Chuck your money into index funds or ETFs, and you're getting a slice of the whole pie. S&P 500? 7% average annual return. 30 years? Over 1,400% growth. Drop that mic!

5. Momentum Investing - The Speedster's Delight.

Ever caught a gust of wind on a bike downhill? That's momentum investing, speed demon! You're surfing market waves and loving every second. It's like catching your opponent off-guard and going in for the win. Tesla? 600% growth in a year. Momentum investors are the cool cats, always chasing the next big rush.

My fellow investment voyager, these five strategies form a multifaceted toolkit that can be tailored to your financial goals and risk tolerance. Just as Kung Fu masters adapt their techniques to different adversaries, you can align these strategies with your aspirations and market conditions. Blend the wisdom of value, growth, income, index, and momentum investing, wielding them with precision and dexterity. With each calculated move, you inch closer to the revered status of an Investment Kung Fu master. Embrace the diversity, train unceasingly, and ascend to the pinnacle of financial expertise! Kapow!

15.3 Investing is Long Term

Greetings, Money master! Knot up that WKF belt, because we're diving deep into the epic world of investing – where time and money high-five to create a combo move more powerful than a Kung Fu master's knockout punch. Get ready to ride the rollercoaster of compounding, because this is the ride you won't want to miss!

Compounding is the ultimate magic trick in this investing circus. Imagine you throw $10,000 into the investment ring with a juicy 15% annual return. After year one, kaboom, you're up by $1,500. Now, here's where the Kung Fu magic happens – in year two, that 15% isn't just on your original cash, it's also on that extra $1,500 you made last year. It's like getting a Kung Fu move that hit twice! And guess what? The longer this dance goes on, the more insane your gains become.

After 10 years of this 15% CAGR, your bag has now blown up from $10,000 to $44,402, a 4.4x return! Fuck, yeah!

And don't you dare think that time is just sitting around twiddling its thumbs. Nah, time is like a Kung Fu sensei, teaching you to read the market's moves. Being a long-term investor is like having your own crystal ball – you can somewhat predict (but not with 100% accuracy, no!) the ups and downs and still come out on top.

But here's the real Kung Fu move – diversification. Just like a Kung Fu warrior with a bunch of killer moves, time lets you spread your investments like Nutella on toast. You're like the superhero of investments, ready to take on anything the market throws your way.

But and this is a big BUT, time isn't doing all the heavy lifting. It's like a Kung Fu training partner – it helps, but you gotta show up at the dojo. Starting your investing journey early is like learning Kung Fu as a kid – you've got the time to perfect your moves and become a true master.

Now, brace yourself for some cold, hard facts. Historically, the S&P 500 – a major US stock index – has given an average annual return of around 7-10%

after adjusting for inflation. Over the past 30 years, it's delivered an impressive cumulative return of over 1,400%. That's like Kung Fu moves that just keep getting better!

So, remember this: time is your secret weapon in the investing game. Let compounding work its voodoo, start your journey early, and use time like a Kung Fu grandmaster uses their staff – with skill and precision. As you journey through the labyrinth of investing, may your wealth grow, your dreams soar, and your legacy shine like a Kung Fu star in the night sky. Pow!

> *SHIPS ARE SAFE IN HARBOUR.*

BUT THAT ISN'T
WHAT SHIPS
ARE FOR.

Chapter 16

The Myths of Investing

16.1 The Myths of Getting Rich

It's time to karate chop the bullshit that's been circulating in the space. Get ready to unlearn as we obliterate these myths that have been swinging nun-chucks of confusion at your investment journey.

16.2 Debunking the Myths

Let's not forget that some myths, while drenched in B.S., might still hold droplets of insight. If they do, and you find they suit your investment sensibilities, by all means adopt or modify. In this rapidly-changing landscape where information and technology are both fast evolving, some myths contain a grain of truth sometimes. Whenever such is the case, apply your flexibility. After all, the final decisions and actions are always yours to make.

Myth 1: Get Rich Quick Schemes.

It is essential to acknowledge the existence of get-rich-quick scams. The infamous Bernie Madoff case is a testament to how these fantasies can crumble into financial nightmares quicker than a soufflé. Remember, building substantial wealth requires dedication, patience, and a solid strategy, not a magical shortcut.

Still, everyday, people fall for such scams, including Forex trading scams that take your money and use that money to pay you back in portions of 6%, 10% or 15%, whichever number gets you to commit. Before that money is fully paid back to you, you can bet some Black Swan event (explained in Volume 1) purportedly happened to the fund, and the scammers now either ask you to deposit more money or simply cease to exist! In such a case, they are the Kung Fu masters practising the dark arts and you have been flipped over in a major smackdown!

Myth 2: **Saving is for Suckers.**

Be careful of this clarion call. If you have never invested and do not plan to, then savings should be your quintessential nest egg for retirement. If you intend to invest, then savings should only cover your emergency fund. The rest should be invested for greater returns. Reckless spending can be as disastrous as a one-legged pirate in a fucking triathlon, and it is this that one must avoid. Striking a balance between spending, saving and investing is your compass to financial prosperity.

Myth 3: **Debt is the Devil, Avoid at all Costs.**

Hold your money horses, debt navigator! While we're waving the "Bullshit" banner, remember that not all debts are harbingers of doom. The student loan crisis is a case in point, as mounting student debt has outpaced car and credit card debt. However, strategic educational borrowing, guided responsibly by a competent professional, can be an investment in future earning potential, provided you wield it with wisdom. A property debt for instance, can be a future asset that creates a new income stream in rentals for your retirement. But the same home loan can turn into a devastating liability if that property goes tenantless for an extended period of time and you find your emergency funds are insufficient to pay the monthly instalments.

The moral of the story is: taking on debt is risky. If you have to take on one, ensure you have more than enough money to service the loan repayments. Otherwise, steer clear away from debts. Debt can be a marvellous leveraging tool to multiply wealth but it is not for everyone. Avoid if you're not sure you can handle it.

Myth 4: Investing is Only for the Rich - You Need Tons of Cash to Start!

Balance your investment equilibrium, WKF warrior! This myth deserves a hefty "Bullshit" stamp. It is sobering to acknowledge that 85% of all millionaires started without wealth. Not having big money is no reason not to have big money! Rome wasn't built in a day.

We spent a whole book in **Wealth Kung Fu Vol 1** explaining how to go from zero to $1 million, starting with a salary! This myth is the kind that the Matrix has used to programme people to remain poor or middle class. This indoctrination, unfortunately, has spawned generation after generation of broke families. To break this insidious chain, one simply has to deliver a knock out punch to this bovine scatology and send it down the toilet hole.

Myth 5: Stock Market is a Casino - You'll Lose Everything!
Steady your investment ship, Captain! While we're dishing out " Bullshit" labels, acknowledge that market volatility is as unpredictable as a weather vane in a hurricane. However, historical data reveal that the average annual return of the S&P 500 from 1950 to 2020 is around 7.3%, debunking the notion that the stock market is a glorified casino.

In the case of Bitcoin, the annualized return as of 1 August 2023, has been a staggering 149% since 2011. The odds of the casino producing millionaires is almost zero. In contrast, the investment markets have produced over 60 million living millionaires across the globe and counting. This myth belongs in the septic tank. It can only be uttered by the intellectually challenged or the downright stupid.

Myth 6: You Need to Be a Financial Genius to Build Wealth. Hold your intellectual grounds, my money master! This is another bullshit card that we have to deal out. While many successful people have the same traits as intelligent people and smart investors, very few are actually geniuses. If this myth were true, every single one of the current 60 million millionaires must be a genius. This is simply not the case.

Myth 7: Success is a Solo Journey - Never Trust Anyone! Ease your scepticism, lone trailblazer! While we're washing away the "B.S." paint, remember that mentorship has proven its value time and again. A survey by SCORE revealed that 93% of entrepreneurs with mentors experienced growth in their businesses. Just as a martial arts master guides an apprentice, wealth mentors can steer you towards victory.

In conclusion, my myth-busting compatriot, let us venture forth into the labyrinth of investment myths with a lantern of discernment. Nourish your scepticism, keep your curiosity sharp, and let critical thinking be your compass. Now, embrace the mindset of an investment detective, armed with wisdom, and navigate the intricate maze of finance with the wisdom of a sage. Hee-yahhh!

16.3 **Customise, Fuck the Rest.**

In the bazaar of wealth-building, you'll encounter a cacophony of well-meaning advisers peddling their universal elixirs. But as a **Wealth Kung Fu** master, you're the architect of your wealth empire. March to your own rhythm, unleash your customized arsenal and send a defiant "Fuck you!" to the status quo. Your wealth, your rules – let the grand symphony of individualization commence! Kapow!

Amidst the chorus of wealth-building advice, remember that you're the composer of your wealth building opus. The principles that resonate with you will create a harmonious melody of prosperity, while the rest can simply fade into the background. Customise your plan. Fuck the rest.

16.4 Your Strategy and Exit Points Are Your Own

Here we decode the secrets of creating your own kickass investment strategy and mastering the art of exit points.

1. Forge Your Vision Like a Badass Blacksmith: Before you leap into the investment battlefield, channel your inner blacksmith and hammer out your goals with the precision of a master craftsman. Are you sprinting like a cheetah for quick wins, or laying down bricks of wealth like a boss architect? Your goals are like the GPS of your investment journey, guiding you toward the treasures you're hunting.

Real-Life Insight: Warren Buffett, the Oracle of Omaha, turned Berkshire Hathaway into a behemoth with a net worth of over $100 billion. His clear vision carved the path to his investment glory. Vision, like a fucking lighthouse, lights the way!

2. Sharpen Your Investment Katana: A true warrior doesn't enter battle with a limp noodle, blindly swinging around like a clueless panda. Oh no, my dear samurai! You gotta sharpen your sword of knowledge. Analyze market trends, devour investment reports, and stay vigilant to the rollercoaster of global shitstorms. Knowledge is your fucking lightsaber, slicing through the darkness of uncertainty!

Real-Life Insight: Ray Dalio, the founder of Bridgewater Associates, rode his knowledge to a net worth of $20 billion. His in-depth research played a vital role in his investment triumph. Knowledge is power, baby!

3. Embrace the Symphony of Diversification: Putting all your golden eggs in one basket is like skydiving without a single parachute. Don't be a fucking clown! Diversify your investments like a maestro conducting a symphony of wealth building awesomeness. Spread your investments across different instruments to create a symphony of success and shield yourself from the shitty impact of a single sour note.

Real-Life Insight: The Harvard Endowment Fund, managed by some financial geniuses, rocked a 12% average annual return over 20 years by spreading their bets. Diversification is about not putting all your eggs in one fragile basket!

4. The Rhythm of Perfect Timing: Timing is like catching a falling star – tricky but oh-so-rewarding! Tune into the market's heartbeat, sense the vibrations, and strike when the cosmos align like a fucking constellation of luck. When a recession arrives, for instance, almost all the markets are down. This is the time to launch your rockets. Patience and impeccable timing are the keys to unlocking the treasure chest of investment wins.

Real-Life Insight: George Soros made a billion-dollar profit by shorting the British pound in the '90s. His impeccable timing was the hammer that shattered the pound's glass house!

5. Plot Your Exit Strategy: Just like a ninja strikes and slips into the shadows, you must plot your exit points like a fucking exit strategy ninja. Don't hang on like a stubborn barnacle when the ship's sinking. Know when to say "Ciao, sucker!" and gracefully slide into a more promising boat.

Real-Life Insight: Steve Jobs pulled off one of the most epic exits and re-entries in history. He got the boot from Apple, launched Pixar, and then returned to make Apple the tech juggernaut it is today. The art of the exit, followed by a triumphant re-entry!

6. The Art of Detachment: Detachment is like embracing the zen of investment. Don't cling to your investments like a desperate lover clutching their last chocolate bar. Learn to let go like a serene monk freeing a caged dove. It's like saying, "Hey, Universe, I trust you!"

Real-Life Insight: John Templeton, the legendary investor, was the Jedi of detachment. His motto: "Invest at the point of maximum pessimism." Embrace detachment, and you'll float above market chaos like a zen master on a cloud!

7. Balance Risk and Reward: Before you dive into the shark-infested ocean of investments, weigh the potential rewards against the nasty bite of risk. If it smells like shit, it's probably shit! Make informed decisions and don't let greed whisper sweet nothings in your ear. Some bonds, shares, properties and most cryptocurrencies should be avoided altogether!

8. Trust Your Inner Investment Sensei: Have faith in your gut instincts, like a wise old owl. Sometimes, your intuition knows more than all the financial experts combined. Tune into your inner compass and navigate your choices with the confidence of a poker player holding a royal flush.

9. Embrace Fucking Mistakes: Even the most fearsome warriors stumble in the heat of battle. Embrace your blunders, for they are the stepping stones to your glory. The path to investment triumph is paved with both victories and defeats. Embrace the chaos and rise like a phoenix from the ashes.

Real-Life Insight: Bill Ackman, the prominent hedge fund manager, famously learned from his failure with Target, which became a cautionary tale. He later bounced back by making strategic adjustments. Learning from blunders for a brighter future!

10. The Dance of Flexibility: The investment realm is as unpredictable as a wild typhoon, and you must be as nimble as a circus acrobat. Be supple in your approach, and don't hesitate to adjust your strategy as the winds of change gust. Agility is an underrated trait in the investment world. The ability to switch assets during the fall of one market and the rise of another is an agile move that few seasoned investors have mastered.

Real-Life Insight: The COVID-19 pandemic disrupted markets worldwide, leading successful investors to pivot their strategies. Companies like Amazon and Zoom witnessed remarkable growth during the crisis, showcasing the importance of adaptability. Investors in equities who cut through the noise would have put swap assets for these tech stocks that eventually rocketed to all time highs post-Covid 19.

There you have it, my intrepid investment warrior! The power to control your strategy and master your exit points lies solely in your capable hands. You are the master of your investment destiny, and no one else can do it for you. Trust in your abilities, embrace the uncertainty, and adapt like a legendary chameleon.

Now, go forth with the fucking confidence, and conquer the investment world with your personalized strategy and impeccable timing. The path to investment glory is yours to create, so seize it with all your might! Kapow!

Chapter 17:

How to Go from $10,000 to $10,000,000

17.1 Find a Fucking Asset with a potential 10x Return

Hey there, money magician! Get ready to strap on your financial jetpack, because we're about to blast off into the stratosphere of turning $10,000 into a jaw-dropping $10,000,000. Yeah, you heard it right – we're talking about turbo-charged multiplication that even a Kung Fu master would envy. So, tighten your Kung Fu belt and get ready to ride the rocket of exponential growth like a true Investment Kung Fu master!

Our first step, my Dragon master, is to track down an asset that's got the mojo for a solid 10x return. But hey, we aren't talking about smoke and mirrors here – this is cold, hard financial math flexing its muscles.

Imagine this: you kickstart the journey with your trusty $10,000, and thanks to the mystical power of a 10x return, that sum transforms into a cool $100,000. Bam! But hold onto your hat, because we're just getting warmed up. With that hefty $100,000 in your pocket, you dive into the next round of financial wizardry, scoring another 10x return that catapults you into the millionaire club with a blazing $1 million! And we're not done yet, my financial comrade. Oh no, not by a long shot.

With that million-dollar war chest, we set our sights higher than a Kung Fu master's jump kick, aiming for the heavens. Another 10x return later, and boom – you're sitting on a colossal $10 million! Can you feel the adrenaline pumping through your veins? That's the pure, unadulterated rush of exponential growth, my friend. When you have truly unfucked your mind from the years of propaganda and lies they have indoctrinated you with, you will start to see the real numbers. Maths doesn't lie!

Now, I know what you're thinking – "Hold up, Master, are we talking unicorns and rainbows here?" And to that, I say, "Hell yeah, we are!" But let me be real with you – this ain't no walk in the park. It's like becoming a Kung Fu grandmaster – it takes smarts, discipline, and a ton of hard work.

So, let's lay down the roadmap to uncovering this mythical 10x asset. It all starts with diving headfirst into the world of research and analysis. Just like a Kung Fu master studying ancient scrolls, we dig deep into stocks, cryptocurrencies, real estate – you name it. We're hunting for those hidden gems that are primed to skyrocket, much like a Kung Fu master's lightning-fast strikes. Maybe it's a disruptive tech startup, a crypto revolution waiting to happen, or a real estate treasure buried in a thriving market.

But, let's not ignore the elephant in the room – risk. Not every asset is going to deliver that dazzling 10x return. Some might fizzle out faster than a firecracker. And that's where the power of diversification swoops in. It's like a Kung Fu sensei with a whole arsenal of moves – we spread our bets across different opportunities, reducing risk and upping our chances of hitting the big leagues.

So, my financial warrior, tighten your belt and prepare for the ride of a lifetime. We're talking about turning a modest sum into a whopping $10,000,000, all while juggling risks and rewards like a true Investment Kung Fu grandmaster. Are you ready for this? Let's unleash the magic and get that motherfucking money flowing!

To provide a tangible glimpse into the potential of this endeavour, feast your eyes on the following chart, which illustrates the power of compounding with a 10x return over 3 times:

Market Cycle	Investment Value
0	$10,000
1	$100,000
2	$1,000,000
3	$10,000,000

Behold the astonishing metamorphosis! In a mere span of 3 market cycles, your initial $10,000 has compounded to a staggering $10 million! This is the true magic of compounding synergized with a 10x return each cycle.

Now, the most obvious asset that has given these orgasmic 10x returns over and over again since inception is none other than Bitcoin! At a reported 1 billion percent return cumulatively since its inception in 2009, this was a 10 million x move!

Now we are not saying history will repeat itself. In fact we are quite sure this gargantuan move will not occur again since the asset is moving away from its nascent, infancy stage. To really analyze and model a realistic price ascension for Bitcoin in 2024 and beyond, many macro-economics cross-factors need to be taken into account. That requires the time and space of an entirely new book! So have Zen-like patience and wait for our Bitcoin volume.

Lastly, engrave the virtue of patience deep within your financial psyche. Just as Kung Fu masters devote years to honing their skills, we too must display unwavering resolve on our investment journey. The grandest fortunes didn't arise overnight. They're the product of steadfast dedication, unyielding perseverance, and unwavering focus. Stay resolute, stand firm against the winds of market volatility, and keep your sights fixed firmly on the ultimate prize.

So, fellow financial crusader, brace yourself for this exhilarating expedition of multiplying returns! Keep your radar keenly attuned to that exceptional asset, wield the power of compounding like a seasoned Investment Kung Fu master, and surge forth with an unshakable resolve, armed with astute strategy and a splash of audacious spirit. Armed with this potent combination, you'll ascend the grand summit of $10,000,000 and emerge victorious on the battleground of wealth! Kapow!

17.2 Preserve Your Fucking Wealth - 10 Ways Millionaires Do It

Brace yourself, financial champion, for you have now conquered the heart-pounding odyssey from $10,000 to an astronomical $10,000,000, wielding the Investment Kung Fu like the true badass warrior you are! But hold onto your motherfucking nunchucks, because the adventure isn't over. Behold the sacred tome that unveils the meticulously curated strategies employed by millionaires to safeguard their fortunes from the treacherous winds of time. It's time to fortify your financial fortress like these motherfucking legends.

1. Diversify: Don't Put All Your Gold in One Chest! Imagine your wealth as a musical symphony – stocks, real estate, gold, and more – each note contributing to a mesmerizing composition. Millionaires aren't betting their entire fortunes on a single tune; they're diversifying their portfolios across different assets. Just as a symphony weaves diverse sounds into an enchanting masterpiece, these financial maestros diversify across various investments, minimizing risk and maximizing returns. Imagine having your cake and eating it too, while dancing to the sweet rhythm of diversified gains! The multimillionaire's portfolio is typically diversified across the board – you will see a strong mix of assets comprising real estate, business, equities, government bonds, gold, silver, cryptocurrencies and perhaps nothing more than 10% in cash.

2. Defensive Stance to Ward Off Financial Shitstorms:
Visualize a Kung Fu warrior adopting a defensive stance, ready to block any sneak attack from a crafty adversary. Similarly, millionaires adopt defensive strategies, allocating a portion of their wealth to low-risk assets like real estate and gold. Just as martial artists brace against incoming blows, these financial protectors shield their

fortunes from market upheavals. When shit hits the fan, they remain unperturbed, firmly rooted like a warrior who isn't letting any financial shitstorm to mess with their stash. Truly defensive assets are hard assets like real estate, gold and bitcoin.

3. Armour Up with Insurance: Don't Be Caught Butt-Naked in the Rain! Think of insurance as your financial armour, shielding you from the shitstorms life may unleash. Millionaires armour up by getting insurance coverage – life, health, property – to safeguard their considerable wealth. Like a warrior suiting up for battle, they don their insurance armour, ready to shield themselves from the shit life can throw at them – health issues, accidents, or natural disasters. They're not caught with their pants down - they're covered!

4. Tax Jujitsu: Flip the Taxman Like a Pancake! Consider taxes as your opponents in a no-holds-barred cage match. Millionaires engage in tax jujitsu, using legal tactics to minimize the motherfucking impact of taxations. They time capital gains, invest in tax-efficient vehicles, and embrace other strategic moves that help them evade taxes. Just as a Kung Fu master uses an opponent's force against them, millionaires can outfox the tax system to maximize their gains. They do this by corporatizing their earnings, writing off most expenses as business expenses that are non-taxable. Those with a competent squadron of accountants and attorneys can be sophisticated enough to use their assets as collaterals for loans that they then use to live off! In the world of best kept secrets amongst the rich, debts are tax-free. But unless you have a professional team of accountants and tax attorneys at your behest, we advise against using debt to build wealth. This is what we opine as the dark arts of wealth-building best left to the Sith Lords!

5. Emergency Arsenal: Whip Out Your Financial Nunchucks! Picture this: You're in a tight spot, so you whip out your nunchucks and show those adversaries who's boss. Millionaires keep an emergency fund, their financial nunchucks, ready to tackle unexpected crises. When shit hits the fan – job loss, medical emergencies, or surprise expenses – they're armed and ready, just like a martial artist who's always prepared for battle.

6. Slash and Burn BS Expenses: Toss 'Em Out Like a Bad Habit! Imagine a Kung Fu master swiftly cutting through distractions, focusing on the heart of the battle. Similarly, millionaires trim bullshit expenses, shedding unnecessary costs that weigh them down. They scrutinize spending, slashing things that add zero value – extravagant dinners, subscription services, or luxury goods, and even relatives and friends who are borrowers! Like a Kung Fu master zeroing in on their opponent's vulnerabilities, millionaires are quick and ruthless in cutting off financially-draining expenses or people!

7. Inflation Annihilation: Beat Inflation to a Pulp! Inflation is like a silent enemy, chipping away at your purchasing power. All WKF masters hate the Number One thief of wealth – Inflation! This is the primary reason why all **Wealth Kung Fu** masters quickly exchange their soft fiat currencies aka cash for hard assets – real estate, commodities, gold, silver, and bitcoin – that historically outpace inflation. Think of it as the very hardened core of **Wealth Kung Fu** – they're beating inflation to a pulp, ensuring their purchasing power remains intact and their wealth keeps growing. Exchanging soft money like fiat currencies for hard assets like gold and bitcoin is like kicking the Matrix in the balls, and getting away with it!

8. The Advisor Avengers: Assemble for Financial Wisdom! Financial advisors are like the Avengers of the financial world – a team of experts coming together to kick financial villains' asses. Millionaires enlist these financial superheroes for advice on investments, taxes, and more. Just as the Avengers bring unique skills to the table, advisors provide valuable insights, ensuring millionaires make sound financial decisions. It's like having your own squad of financial Avengers, ready to take down any financial foe.

9. Estate Legacy: Pass Down Your Kung Fu Wisdom! Think of estate planning as passing down your **Wealth Kung Fu** techniques to future generations. Millionaires craft detailed plans to ensure their wealth smoothly transitions to heirs and beneficiaries. They create wills, trusts, and designations, like a Kung Fu master passing on their techniques to worthy successors. By mastering the art of estate planning, millionaires ensure their financial legacy endures, continuing to thrive for generations to come.

10. Precision Planning: Every Move's a Calculated Strike! In the world of wealth preservation, millionaires execute each financial move with precision, like a masterful Kung Fu technique. Whether it's adjusting investments, rebalancing portfolios, or fine-tuning financial strategies, every move is calculated for maximum impact. This meticulous approach ensures millionaires remain unwavering in their quest for enduring financial triumphs.

With these mighty strategies in your arsenal, you stand as the unyielding guardian of your $10,000,000 kingdom. Embrace diversification, shield with defensive postures, armour up with insurance, flip the motherfucking tax game, slash unnecessary costs and even cut out financially-draining parasites (ie. people). Beat inflation to a pulp, assemble your financial Avengers, pass down your legacy, and execute each move with precision.

Remember, this is an ongoing quest; adapt, refine, and continue to wield your **Wealth Kung Fu** with skill and finesse. As you fortify your financial fortress, rest assured that your $10,000,000 legacy will shine brightly for generations, a testament to your financial badassery. Kapow!

17.3 Wealth-Building vs. Wealth-Preservation

Get ready for the ultimate smackdown: Wealth-Building vs. Wealth-Preservation! Imagine this as the showdown of the century, where two Kung Fu legends step into the ring, each armed with their unique moves and ready to unleash some serious ***Wealth Kung Fu***.

In one corner, we've got the gutsy and audacious Wealth-Builder – the daredevil aiming to pump up their fortunes like there's no tomorrow. And in the other corner, meet the suave and tactical Wealth-Preserver – the cool cat looking to guard their treasures like a true Kung Fu master protecting their ancient scrolls. It's on, my friend, and you're about to witness the ultimate financial face-off!

Hold onto your seat as we explore the wild ride known as Wealth-Building! Think of this as a blockbuster action flick, complete with adrenaline-pumping stunts and heart-stopping twists. Wealth-Builders are like the stunt doubles of finance, leaping headfirst into opportunities like Kung Fu acrobats soaring through the air.

They thrive on risk, seizing chances with the intensity of a ninja striking in the dark. It's like watching a Kung Fu master pull off jaw-dropping moves that make you yell, "Holy shit, did you see that?" These warriors are hungry for those explosive gains and aren't afraid to dive into the market chaos with all guns blazing. But, dear comrade, just as a Kung Fu hero needs to nail their complex flips, a Wealth-Builder must stay sharp and nimble, ready to pivot on a dime. The name of their game is risk. Remember risk-reward ratio? Remember looking for that 10x return? Wealth-builders are aggressive risk-takers!

Now, let's flip the script and meet our second contender: Wealth-Preservation! Imagine a sophisticated Kung Fu guru sipping tea while chaos erupts around them. That's the vibe of Wealth-Preservation.

This Dragon master is like the wise old Kung Fu sage who has seen it all and knows how to protect themselves without breaking a sweat. They keep it cool, spreading their assets like a ninja with a trunk full of disguises, always ready to switch tactics in a heartbeat. If the financial world were a turbulent sea, Wealth-Preservation would be the seasoned captain who navigates the rough waters like it's a Sunday stroll. They're all about taming risk, securing their riches, and steering their ship to calm water. The name of the game here is preserving. Wealth-preservers are not looking for 10x or 100x returns. They thrive in calm water. They look for safe harbour. A low-risk, low-reward environment to preserve that $10 million is the paramount objective. Their aim is not to grow their $10 million to $100 million by investing in a potential 10x asset!

But hold your horses, my money warrior! Here's the plot twist: you don't have to pick a side! Yup, you heard that right. You've got the power to dance between both worlds like a Kung Fu master who rocks both nunchucks and staff. You can be a dual force, swinging between the thrilling offense of Wealth-Building and the solid defence of Wealth-Preservation like a true master. Sometimes you'll be soaring through the air like a praying mantis, chasing those sky-high returns. Other times, you'll be holed up in your financial dojo, deflecting volatility like a Kung Fu maestro guarding their temple.

Here's the golden ticket: your wealth journey is as unique as a signature Kung Fu move. It's about finding that sweet spot that matches your style, risk appetite, and financial dreams. You're not locked into one strategy – you can blend the fire of Wealth-Building with the ice of Wealth-Preservation to choreograph your own wealth adventure. So, my financial gladiator, step into the arena and make your own mark. Be fearless, be smart, and be ready to unleash some epic ***Wealth Kung Fu***! Now go, and script your legendary saga! Kapow!

Strategy	Wealth-Building	Wealth-Preservation
Risk Approach	High-octane pursuit of explosive growth	Reducing risk to a minimal with preservation of wealth as key focus
Tactical	Seizing opportunities for massive gains	Safeguarding against market turmoil
Investment Mantra	High-risk, high-reward investments	Diversification, risk minimization
Time Horizon	Short to medium-term	Long-term stability and security
Risk Tolerance	High	Low to moderate
Standout Benefit	Jaw-dropping gains that leave you speechless	Sleep-at-night confidence
Notable Challenge	High volatility, potential for major losses	Potentially lower returns compared to high-risk
Best Suited For	Risk-loving thrill-seekers	Prudent, risk-averse investors
Example	Investing in startups, high-growth stocks, cryptocurrencies.	Real estate, gold, Bitcoin

(Note: The table provides an expanded comparison of Wealth-Building and Wealth-Preservation strategies, showcasing key features, benefits, challenges, and examples for each approach.)

Chapter 18:

Daily Habits
of the Unfucked Mind

18.1 Introduction

Greetings, noble investment warrior! In this expansive chapter, we embark on a journey as riveting as any legendary Kung Fu saga, and I'm not talking about the sugar-coated bullshit that some 'gurus' sell. No, we're bringing you the real deal, the unfiltered, unvarnished truth about mastering the art of **Wealth Kung Fu**. So, sit down, pour yourself that cuppa of Kwan Yin tea, and get ready to discover the secret scrolls of "The Daily Habits of the Unfucked Mind," a path to wealth mastery that involves a daily regimen of practices and rituals. Just as martial artists hone their skills through ceaseless practice, wealth mastery requires a set of disciplined daily habits. In this chapter, we explore the intricate art of these habits, which can transform you into a true WKF sage.

18.2 Defining the Winner's Daily Investment Kung Fu

The Winner's Daily Investment Kung Fu transcends mere investing; it is the path to mastering the art of wealth accumulation one day at a time, and let me tell you, it's a journey, not a quick shag. Visualise this as a martial artist perfecting their ancient techniques every single day, forging not just their body but their investment mind. These daily rituals form the backbone of your investment training regimen, moulding your mindset and sculpting your investment acumen.

So, if after positioning yourself in the assets market, you plan to sit on your palms, you're in the wrong fucking place. But if you're ready to embark on a journey of daily commitment, discipline, and financial skill-building, then welcome to the Winner's Daily Investment Kung Fu. It's the real deal that will transform you into an investment master, one day at a time.

We are asking you to level up, dear WKF master! Make this winner's mindset an inextricable part of you. Because your daily habits define your character. Your character defines your destiny. Picture Yoda and Luke nodding in approval right now! Yes! Ohm.

18.3 Components of the Winner's Daily Investment Kung Fu

1. Goal Setting: Your Financial Battle Plan: Picture this as the morning preparation of a Kung Fu fighter. Setting clear investment objectives is your key to investment combat. We're not talking just about lofty long-term goals but daily and weekly targets too. An investment warrior without a daily ritual of habits is akin to a ronin without a master, and that's just a recipe for disaster, and nobody wants that shitshow. Maybe your WKF goal this week is to incur no credit card debt whatsoever. Maybe your daily goal this month is to buy into any price weakness in the XRP and Solana markets as part of your larger accumulation strategy. Whatever it is, little daily goals become your habits. Habits become your character. Character becomes your destiny!

2. Continuous Learning: Wax On, Wax Off. Like a martial artist refining their motherfucking hand-waxing skills daily, you must invest time in reading as many motherfucking non-fiction books as possible. And after you've done that, repeat! Poor people do not learn, and hence they do not earn! The rich learn. Then they earn. Financial markets are a realm of constant flux, and you must learn and adapt to stay ahead. Every day, you must strive to acquire new knowledge, whether it's about a specific stock, a market trend, or a novel market innovation. Your daily learning routine mirrors the "Wax On, Wax Off" principle of your investment Kung Fu, and it's no shoddy shortcut, it's the real deal. Remember, the mind that continuously learns is what separates the rich from the poor!

3. Financial Chi Tracking: Your daily financial Chi tracking is akin to mindful eating, but for your finances. It's about being keenly aware of every fucking Benjamin that flows into or out of your wallet. This daily ritual cultivates a heightened sense of financial awareness, empowering you to detect and address financial leaks swiftly. No shifty business here, we're talking about cold, hard awareness. To not track your financial ins and outs daily is like a pilot flying blind without looking at his instruments. Eventually, that can only lead him into one direction – down.

4. Savings Dojo: Just as a martial artist builds strength and endurance through rigorous training, you are constructing your wealth one contribution at a time. Your daily savings practice mirrors the dojo where you train, and each contribution is akin to a punch you unleash. While it might appear inconsequential in the short term, over time, it assembles the wealth-building strength necessary to confront any financial challenge. This unglamorous daily grind of the secret millionaire is like that opening scene in John Wick 4. John, in his dungeon, shirtless and powerful, all fucking 100% masculine, throwing punch after punch onto a block of wood till his fists bleed. This is the daily training. Make yourself hard to kill. In real combat, somebody's gonna die, baby! And it ain't you.

5. Writing your own Kung Fu scrolls: Regularly recording, updating and reviewing your investments are weekly habits worthy of a real WKF master. This is YOU writing your own daily Kung Fu scrolls, my master! Write it all down. In a good old fashioned notebook. Hard copy, yes! Or in your tablet, we don't fucking care.

Previous capital? New capital? Buy? Sell? Profit? Loss? Percentage of return? Average buying price? Average selling price? Percentage of gold in your portfolio? Percentage of Microsoft shares in your portfolio? Percentage of dry powder aka cash? Percentage of Ethereum?

Remember, this is your opus. You are the author of your wealth! Ain't nobody is gonna write that shit for you. And they shouldn't be made to.

These are your treasures. keep them as secrets. Tuck them away in a dark, safe place. Like motherfucking John Wick tucking his gold coins and guns away, man! When you finally take them out, it looks so hot and sexy!

So, as you dive into your Winner's Daily Investment Kung Fu habits, remember that these components are your daily practice, not some theoretical bullshit. It's the real substance behind your wealth mastery. The poor and the middle-class have no such habits. And without small, daily and weekly goals and wins, they have no inkling of what big wins or victories even taste like. Their victim mentality lays further siege in their minds and this is why "life happens" to them. The rich count on no such self-pity or self-delusion. If they want something, they will focus all their thoughts, energy and effort into making it happen! The unfucked mind is truly a beautiful thing! Quiet. Observant. Knowing. Focussed. Disciplined. Defence-ready. Attack-ready. Unkillable!

18.4 Benefits of the Winner's Daily Investment Kung Fu

Why embrace the Winner's Daily Investment Kung Fu? Because it's the gateway to investment mastery.

- **Investment Discipline:** Just as a martial artist hones their technique, these daily habits sharpen your investment discipline. No mucking about, this is the real deal, and you live, breath and sleep WKF. Repeat. WKF is not just a mindset. It's a lifestyle for the secret millionaire.

- **Investment Knowledge and Confidence:** The Winner's Daily Investment Kung Fu bolsters your investment wisdom and confidence. It's like ascending to a higher Kung Fu belt; you become more self-assured and better equipped to face investment adversaries. Read. Read. Read. Learn something everyday. Every morsel of new knowledge you see, feed it into your head. When your mind is strong, your body and your actions follow, man. Your whole WKF self becomes a weapon of mass destruction! Fuck, yeah!

- **Progress Towards Mastery:** Each day spent practising your Winner's Daily Investment Kung Fu is a stride towards long-term investment mastery. It's like the daily training of a martial artist, who consistently refines their skills. Mastery is after all not about practising 1,000 kicks one time but about practising one kick 1,000 times.

- **Enhanced Risk Management and Decision-Making:** Risk management is your shield and sword. It's akin to a martial artist who anticipates their opponent's moves and reacts swiftly. Your daily risk management practice keeps you agile and sharp, no smoke and mirrors here.

So, if you're wondering why you should give a flying fuck about the Winner's Daily Investment Kung Fu, these benefits are your answer. It's a tried and tested path to the Promised Land. And the millionaire's mindset is a Winner's Mindset.

18.5 Facing Dragons and Defying Gravity

Implementing the Winner's Daily Investment Kung Fu can be as daunting as confronting a formidable dragon for the uninitiated. It's not all serene gardens and cherry blossoms; there may be fierce challenges to overcome. But fear not, for every obstacle conceals a path to triumph. In this chapter, we offer practical tips for surmounting these challenges and maintaining the consistency required to excel in your Winner's Daily Investment Kung Fu. No bullshit, just real strategies to overcome real challenges. You'll encounter obstacles in your investment journey, but with the right strategies and mindset, you can overcome them and continue on your path to investment mastery.

So, if you're ready to face the dragons of financial uncertainty and defy the gravity that holds others down, this chapter is your guide. It's about equipping you with the skills and mindset to navigate the challenges that may come your way and emerge victorious on the other side. It's not always going to be a walk in the park, but it sure as hell is worth it.

Chapter 19:

The Winner's Portfolio

Here we are, WKF master. Almost at the end of this Volume. In this dojo, The Winners have honed their financial martial arts to $10,000,000 perfection. Here, we'll unveil The Winner's Portfolio, explore their favourite assets, dive into their pros and cons, and learn what to do next.

19.1 The Wisdom behind the Winner's Moves

Before we dive into The Winner's choice of assets, let's peek behind the curtain and see how they invest.

- **Diversification:** The cornerstone of The Winner's strategy is diversification. It's like a martial artist mastering a broad spectrum of techniques. They spread their wealth across various asset classes, reducing risk. A portion goes into stocks for growth, gold for stability, cryptocurrencies for exponential returns, alternative assets for uniqueness, and cash for flexibility.

- **Long-Term Vision**: The Winner is not in it for a quick buck. They're like the martial artist who knows that mastery takes time. They invest with a long-term vision. Compound interest and the gradual appreciation of assets are their trusted allies.

- **Continuous Learning:** The Winner is a voracious learner, like a Kung Fu master who keeps refining their techniques. They stay informed about the financial world, monitor market trends, and adapt their strategies. Investing in knowledge, they say, pays the best interest.

- **Risk Management:** In the financial martial arts, the name of the game is risk management. The Winner allocates their investments according to their risk tolerance and investment goals. They're not out to conquer the world; they want to secure their future.

- **Regular Review:** Like a martial artist evaluating their performance, The Winner regularly reviews their portfolio. They rebalance to maintain the desired asset allocation and ditch underperforming assets. It's all about staying in top financial shape.

Now, armed with this knowledge, let's delve into The Winners's favourite assets and see how they've mastered each one.

19.2 Dipping Balls into Crypto

We kick things off with a battlefield that's sent shockwaves through the world of investments since 2009 – cryptocurrencies. These digital wonders, like Bitcoin and Ethereum, are like the secret weapons of The Unfucked Mind. The question is, should they be yours too?

Pros:

High Growth Potential: Let's get real with some numbers that'll make your head spin like a Kung Fu roundhouse kick. Imagine you'd invested just $100 in Bitcoin back in 2011. By 2021, that pocket change would've been worth over $4.6 million! That's like turning your grandma's antique teapot into a Picasso original. If that's not the "Holy shit, I'm rich!" moment, we don't fucking know what is. The cryptocurrency market cap hit a colossal $2 trillion in 2021.

Decentralization: In a world where central banks and governments often pull the financial strings, cryptocurrencies are like practicing a martial art without a master; you're the sole master of your moves. Bitcoin, in particular, is mined through a decentralized network of computers, making it impervious to central control.

Global Currency: You know how martial artists transcend borders with their skills? Cryptocurrencies. Cryptocurrencies are light years ahead of those motherfucking fiat currencies. They travel at the speed of light in the Internet, yo! On that score, not only can you send and receive money digitally, you can do so across the whole motherfucking planet. We are portable across space and time here. Dump that fiat because it's old, losing value everyday and so fucking slow!

Just a word of caution that there are some 20,000 cryptos in the digital space. 99.9% have no use-case and will go to zero! Only a handful of majors have fundamentals. For the record, we only give our attention, not warranty motherfucker, to:Bitcoin, Ethereum, Solana and Ripple XRP. This does not mean that they won't go to zero! We make no such claim! The possibility of all assets going to zero is above zero percent, if you ask us. That goes for the US Dollar too! Nothing is 100%. Nothing is certain, except death and taxes.

Cons:

Volatility: Now, cryptocurrencies don't just waltz through the financial markets; they somersault, cartwheel, and often belly flop. Their prices have swung from around a fraction of a penny in 2010 to over $60,000 in 2021. That's like a Kung Fu battle where combatants strike with unpredictable moves, fly up into the air like motherfucking vampires, and in mid-air, cut each other's balls off. Spectacular. In a week, you can gain a fortune or suffer a devastating loss. Bitcoin's price surged to over $63,000 in April 2021, only to plummet to around $16,000 at the end of 2022.

Regulatory Challenges: If you think mastering a martial art is tough, try understanding the labyrinth of cryptocurrency regulations. The regulatory environment for these digital currencies is still evolving, akin to navigating a new and uncharted territory. In the UK, the Financial Conduct Authority (FCA) only started regulating crypto firms in early 2020. In the United States, the SEC (Securities Exchange Commission) at the time of writing is enforcing by litigations when it comes to digital assets. It's a shitshow, to put it mildly. Globally, countries are still formulating and/or flip-flopping their stances on cryptocurrency regulations, leading to a high degree of uncertainty.

Crypto Bankruptcies List: TerraUSD. Genesis Global Capital. FTX. BlockFi. Celsius Network. Voyager Digital. Three Arrows Capital. Gemini Trust. These are not all but some of the most notable cryptocurrency companies that filed for bankruptcy.

The reason for each crypto company bankruptcy is complex, but in general the crypto bankruptcies in 2022 followed the collapse of TerraUSD and FTX. Many crypto exchanges and lenders are interconnected, with each company's liquidity depending on investments and loans in other companies.

When these bankruptcies happen, investors face losing all their investments. Be cognisant of this very high risk of storing your digital assets in digital exchanges or any crypto custodian. This counter-party risk cannot be ignored by any investor!

For crypto investors, the cliche "Not your key, not your crypto" is a clarion call for the community to take their private keys off crypto exchanges and into self custody. We shall go into details of this somewhat complex procedure in Volume 3.

Hacking Risks: While cryptocurrencies are like the secret weapons of The Winners, they face the risk of hacking when they reside in digital exchanges and crypto custodian parties. Cryptocurrencies are susceptible to hacking. In 2019, for instance, a major exchange, Binance, suffered a hack that cost them $40 million.

19.3 Alternative Assets

Now, let's delve into the intriguing world of alternative assets. The Winners don't limit themselves to conventional investments; they venture into the obscure and the eccentric, much like martial artists who explore unusual combat styles. These assets, including Rolex, Patek Philippe, fine wines, and art, are novelties, rarities and collectibles that base their values on largely one factor - scarcity.

Pros:

Potential for Staggering Returns: These unconventional assets have the potential to appreciate significantly. It's like finding out your grandma's attic is a treasure trove filled with hidden Picasso paintings, and you exclaim, "Holy shit, I'm rich!" For instance, a rare Patek Philippe watch can see an increase of 100% to 300% in the aftermarket, outperforming many traditional investments. In the fine wine world, a bottle that costs you a couple of hundred dollars today might fetch you thousands in a few years. No kidding!

Tangible Elegance: These investments are a far cry from mere numbers on a screen. They're tangible assets, like owning the Mona Lisa, but in financial form. Owning a valuable painting or a fine watch isn't just about the figures; it's about what I have that you can't have even when we're both millionaires or billionaires.

Diversification Ninja: Conventional investments follow a set of rules, like a traditional martial art form. But alternative assets dance to the beat of their own drums. They offer unique and uncorrelated returns, injecting an element of surprise into the Winner's portfolio. It's like having an ace up your sleeve in a high-stakes card game. When everything else is hanging in the balance, your alternative assets might just be your hidden Royal Flush.

Cons:

Specialized Expertise Required: Don't think diving into alternative assets is a walk in the park. No, no! Understanding these assets requires more than just a passing interest. You need to have professorial knowledge in this esoteric world. A notable example is art authentication, where the expertise of seasoned art historians plays a pivotal role.

Liquidity Conundrums: The unconventional assets don't play by the rules of the stock market. Liquidity can fluctuate like a rollercoaster in a financial amusement park. Selling these assets isn't as simple as clicking "sell" on a stock trading app. It's more like trying to sell your vintage vinyl record collection in a world obsessed with Spotify and Apple Music. It's not exactly a thriving market, and you might exclaim, "What's the deal with this shit?" Fine watches, for instance, might be purchased in the grey market due to high demand and long waiting lists at authorised dealers.

So, dear investor, you've now ventured deeper into the world of The Winner's Portfolio. The path is never straightforward, but it's full of intrigue, allure, and the potential for vast riches. Will you join The Winner's mindset? What would the portfolio of the Unfucked Mind look like? There is no hard or fast rule. Investment is not a science. It is an art. The portfolio is yours to craft and the adventure is yours for the taking.

ASSET	PORTFOLIO ALLOCATION	EXPECTED CAGR
REAL ESTATE	50%	4%
NASDAQ	10%	15%
GOLD	4%	4%
SILVER	1%	6%
LUXURY WATCHES	10%	7%
XRP	2%	20%
SOLANA	2%	75%
BITCOIN	21%	50%

*CAGR is Compounded Annual Growth Rate.

This table is solely the author's personal calculations. It is not financial advice nor a warranty. Nothing is 100% certain. Any investment asset price can fall to zero. Any investment risk you take is yours and yours only.

Chapter 20:

Staying Wealthy and Unfucked from hereon

20.1 Protecting the Fortress of Wealth

Greeting, my dear WKF master. We have reached the last chapter of this volume. We find ourselves at the culmination of our epic quest for investment wisdom. In this chapter, we unveil the hidden scrolls of how the true champions of wealth not only amass great fortunes but also secure and perpetuate them for generations. Just as a martial artist must not only master attacks but also defend against them, an investment warrior must safeguard their wealth. In a world rife with financial adversaries, this chapter explores the ancient art of wealth preservation.

In the realm of investment, preservation is as vital as accumulation. As much as we focus on amassing wealth, we must equally focus on preserving it from potential threats and adversaries. The journey of a financial warrior is not just about gaining riches, it's about ensuring that these riches endure, providing financial security not just for yourself but for future generations.

20.2 **Risk Management Recalibrated**

Now, let's dive deep into the guardians of your investments, your risk management strategies. Think of them as your arsenal of defensive martial arts moves for your investment portfolio. Just as a skilled fighter adapts their techniques to counter different attacks, as an investor, you need to employ various strategies to protect your investments.

One of the key strategies in your arsenal is diversification. It's like having a range of martial arts techniques at your disposal. Recent data and studies confirm the effectiveness of diversification in reducing portfolio risk and volatility. It's not just some empty promise, this strategy is grounded in real-life statistics.

Diversification involves spreading your investments across various defensive, risk-off assets like real estate, gold, silver, and Bitcoin. The idea is simple: if one investment performs poorly, others may perform better, balancing out your overall risk. Recent data from reputable financial sources reveals how diversification has been a successful shield against market downturns and extreme volatility.

For instance, during the 2008 financial crisis, diversified portfolios weathered the storm better than those heavily invested in a single asset class. It's a tried and tested strategy to protect your wealth from any Black Swan event (we discussed this in detail in WKF Vol 1) and from market upheavals. Remember, at this stage you are no longer aggressively building wealth. You are protecting it.

Another strategy in your risk management arsenal if you are still in equities (something we do not recommend as a wealth protection strategy) is setting stop-loss orders. They're designed to limit your losses if an investment starts going south. Real-life statistics back this up; studies show that setting stop-loss orders is an effective way to mitigate losses when an investment takes a downturn.

By setting stop-loss orders and implementing a well-thought-out asset allocation strategy, you're essentially creating a financial fortress. So, arm yourself with this strategy, and may your investments be as resilient as a fortress. Your investments are your legacy; protect them wisely.

20.3 Keeping The Thieves at bay

Taxes, the stealthy adversary, constantly lurk in the shadows. Yet, much like a ninja, you can manoeuvre through the intricate world of taxes.

Let's not dance around it. Taxes are a financial ninja's worst enemy, silently chipping away at your hard-earned money. This isn't the time for half-baked strategies or bogus advice. You need the real deal, and that's a team of highly competent tax accountant and tax attorney. Nevermind if that team consists of only two experts. Customize the size of this team according to the size of your wealth and the complexities of the work.

Recent statistics from reliable financial sources demonstrate that individuals who employ effective tax planning strategies can save a significant percentage of their income compared to those who neglect this aspect of their wealth preservation. The data speak for themselves and underscore the critical role of intelligent tax management in wealth preservation.

20.4 **Estate Planning**

Just as a wise master passes down their teachings to their devoted disciples, you have the power to ensure your investment legacy benefits your heirs. We're delving into the world of estate planning, a time-honoured method for preserving your wealth and passing it on to secure your family's future.

Recent data from research tell a compelling story. These data showcase how individuals who have put in the effort to structure their estates thoughtfully have managed to avoid hefty legal fees and minimise their tax obligations. This is about preserving your wealth for your loved ones.

So, pay attention Dragon master. This is where your investment journey takes on a new level of meaning. It's time to secure your legacy, protect your wealth, and ensure your family's financial future is a bright one.

20.5 Staying Informed, Continuous Learning & Staying Unfucked

In Kung Fu, daily practice sharpens your skills. Similarly, in wealth management, staying informed is paramount. This will serve as your daily stay-fit habit. For instance, given the bamboozling from hackers and dodgy exchanges that are still currently prevalent in the crypto-verse, not staying informed is a nincompoop's game. Unless of course, you have taken out your Bitcoin stack from exchanges and stored it in a cold wallet!

You see, like in Kung Fu, knowledge and awareness are your greatest allies in the world of investments where fuckeries are aplenty. Not keeping up with accurate, updated information and new knowledge is a sure way to suffer losses!

Recent statistics back this up, demonstrating that those who keep learning and stay in the know are more likely to navigate the investment markets successfully. In this ever-changing landscape, your knowledge and awareness are your most important weapons. It's about being prepared so that you're not caught off guard when a market shitstorm appears.

Continue to read books and learn from whatever digital platforms that are relevant. Nurture that beautiful mind and stay unfucked from the propaganda and bullshit churned out by the government, the banks, and their lapdogs, and the mainstream media.

20.6 Stand Prepared for the Coming Collapse of Everything

As you complete your journey in Vol 2, it's essential to prepare, at least mentally at this nascent stage, for what's coming. And what's coming is not always pretty or easy to deal with. But with knowledge (again!) and continuous updates of information, you shall once again make yourself unkillable!

1. Simultaneous Explosions of Technological Disruptions:
For the first time in modern human history, simultaneous explosions in technological disruptions are going to happen. Artificial Intelligence (AI), Robotics, Genomics, Blockchain, Clean Energy, Nanotechnology, and Space Exploration are all being rapidly developed or redeveloped right now, all at the same time. Each will result in fundamental changes to our lives, socially, economically, and even politically.

In fact, the detonation of AI into our reality has already happened. In these coming few years, we will see an acceleration of AI development so much so that it will end in Singularity, the point at which AI gives birth to new AI, each one more intelligent than the previous (unlike humans), resulting in the culmination of a Superintelligence that either helps humanity move up the Kardashev Scale (we are currently not even Type 1!) or simply ends us! That's the hypothesis presently.

For the WKF master, who is one of the wisest sub-species of humanity, AI ending humanity is not a major concern. Unlike the bottom 99%, we know this 3 dimensional world is but a temporary state of existence. Ascension to a higher dimension awaits. A parallel Universe awaits. Heck, a copious amount of Multiverse awaits! Go talk to a quantum physicist!

So, before all this happens, let's stay rooted in our present reality. What are your next 3 moves, WKF master? Answer: Look for the next alpha asset to invest! Then invest. Then wait. Brilliant, innit?

We will go into this in greater details in Vol 3. You cannot afford not to read it!

2. Web3.0: While losers continue their habit of spending their remaining days on Earth with their five low-value friends who cannot help them improve their lives, the WKF master must now train their sight on the behemoth looming over humanity - Web 3.0.

We implore you to ditch even other millionaires and billionaires in your life temporarily and set time aside to study this!

While 99% of this digital space has not yet been developed, what we do know is this:

1. *You will have more autonomy*

2. *Your personal data can be protected*

3. *You don't have to sell your privacy*

4. *You can use an avatar to work, play and transact*

5. *Blockchain integration will happen*

6. *Cryptocurrencies will be used*

7. *Decentralized groups will emerge*

8. *Centralized social media will weaken*

9. *New streams of income will emerge*

10. *New millionaires and billionaires will be minted here*

Any of you harbouring bad Boomer or Gen X habits like getting spooked by new tech is not going to make it! Unfuck your mind, please! It's so easy to learn new things now. So, go learn!

Web3 is coming, whether you like it or not. And a shitload of money is going to be made here!

3. Stand Prepared for the Coming Collapse of Everything:

Now, my esteemed money master, the end of this journey is not the final chapter. It's the beginning of your wealth legacy looking at the dawn of something even more exciting coming your way. The fucked mind cannot see this. 99% of the world population are still not awake. In the forthcoming volume in our WKF series, we shall deep-dive into the brave new world of technological disruptions, the coming collapse of fiat currencies, the global shitstorm of a motherfucking sovereign debt crisis, the fall of central banks, the annihilation of traditional banking, and the rise of Bitcoin. All of these shall greatly benefit the Wealth Kung Fu master who stands prepared. Afterall, $900 trillion worth of global wealth facing shifting seismic tremors on the global financial landscape has to benefit some people. Let that some people be you! Kapow! Ka-Ching! Ka-Ching! Ka-Ching!

PEOPLE WHO BOUGHT THIS
BOOK ALSO BOUGHT THE OTHER
TWO BOOKS. MAKE SURE YOUR

WKF COLLECTION

IS COMPLETE.

WEALTH KUNG FU VOL 1	WEALTH KUNG FU VOL 2	**WEALTH KUNG FU VOL 3**
ZERO TO 1 MILLION	*UNFUCK YOUR MIND*	*FIAT FUCKERY VS BITCOIN BADASSERY*

BUY AT *WEALTHKUNGFU.COM*